Why You Behave in Ways You Hate

AND WHAT YOU CAN DO ABOUT IT

Irwin Gootnick, M.D.

Penmarin Books
Granite Bay, California

Editorial Offices:	*Sales and Customer Service Offices:*
Penmarin Books	Midpoint Trade Books
2011 Ashridge Way	27 West 20th Street, Suite 1102
Granite Bay, CA 95746	New York, NY 10011
	(212) 727-0190

Penmarin Books are available at special discounts for bulk purchases for premiums, sales promotions, or education. For details, contact the Publisher. On your letterhead, include information concerning the intended use of the books and how many you wish to purchase.

Printed in Canada
1 2 3 4 5 6 7 8 9 10   04 03 02 01 00

Library of Congress Cataloging-in-Publication Data

Gootnick, Irwin.
  Why you behave in ways you hate : and what you can do about it /
  Irwin Gootnick.
       p.   cm.
  Includes index.
  ISBN 1-883955-18-1 (paperback)
  1. Behavior modification.   2. Problem solving.   3. Change
(Psychology)   I. Title.
BF637.B4G66   1997
158—dc21   97-27952

DEDICATED TO MY FAMILY:

My son JORDAN, an expert in computers, who helped me to master computer technology and word processing.

My daughter JENNIFER, a budding writer, who helped with editing and made a number of valuable suggestions.

My wife SUSAN, who reviewed the manuscript and provided enthusiastic support for my efforts.

CONTENTS

PREFACE

There seems to be a universal and powerful interest in the subject of why people become unhappy and remain trapped in unwanted behaviors in spite of their best efforts not to. Has the explosion of self-help and psychology books, with their myriad theories and paths to change, helped people to better understand and solve their problems?

My goal in writing this book was to go beyond general information and provide people with the knowledge of how and why their specific problems and self-destructiveness developed, and to understand and overcome the hidden mental forces that prevent them from getting free of behaviors they hate.

I want to express my appreciation to Dr. Joseph Weiss, an original thinker, inspirational teacher, and friend for many years. Some of the concepts in my book were influenced by a number of his ideas. Many of the applications are based on my thirty years of clinical experience and teaching.

Also, I would like to thank Mona Riley for helping me to achieve a more fluid and hopefully more lively writing style. In addition, she provided valuable suggestions about the organization of the material in the book.

IRWIN GOOTNICK, M.D.

CHAPTER ONE

Why You Behave in Ways You Hate

AS A CHILD, DID YOU PROMISE yourself that when you grew up you would avoid your parents' worst qualities, only to realize at some point in your adult life that you were behaving just like them? Have you ever wondered why?

Do you hate yourself for being susceptible to salespeople who want you to buy products you don't want or need? Do you wonder why it's difficult for you to turn down requests for money, or requests in general? Or conversely, are you the type of person who has to say no to any request or suggestion, even when it's in your interest to go along? These are examples of being compelled to behave in ways you may despise in spite of your desire and best efforts not to.

On the other hand, you may have wondered why people seem to comfortably behave in ways that undermine their best interests, and only later hate themselves for it. Almost everyone knows about overindulging in decadent foods in spite of weight and other health problems. The remorse that follows seldom seems to diminish the pleasure of the moment, or to keep us from overindulging again. The promise to ourselves to do better the next time is rarely followed and barely appeases our sense of guilt for having failed again.

Similarly, you may know people who routinely party or watch TV in order to distract themselves from important tasks such as schoolwork or their job. Although these and other self-defeating activities may feel great at the time, the regret that follows is usually painful, although not sufficient to change the self-defeating pattern.

Failure in achieving success is a major source of distress for many people. Does career or school success elude you? Do you undermine yourself after achieving success in school or at work, or do you prevent yourself from becoming successful in the first place? Did you drop out of school, even though you thought you wanted to be someone? Have you found that you are unable to achieve success in spite of having talent and opportunity?

Do your problems with success revolve around money? Many people habitually lose money when investing, even though they have years of experience and have read everything on the subject. It may surprise you to know that many experienced professional traders and money managers consistently lose money. There are also those who repeat the pattern of making a great deal of money, then losing it. They don't learn from their negative experiences. Do you have similar conflicts with success?

Many people are plagued by negative behavior and thoughts that affect their ability to be liked and to feel good about themselves. Are you, for example, unable to accept compliments or allow yourself ever to be the center of attention? Do people reject you because you act antagonistically towards them? Does that cause you to change? Do these patterns persist, even though you vow that you will try to change?

Perhaps you are one of those individuals who criticize themselves excessively. For example, are you plagued with thoughts like "I'm a baby" (or stupid, lazy, no good, weak, unappealing), but can't get them out of your mind?

Some people dislike themselves for not being able to have successful relationships. Do you know people who repeatedly date men or women who make them miserable, or who have difficulty leaving a bad relationship? What about people who get mad when their spouse or lover is accommodating and nice to them? Are you terrific at seducing someone of the opposite sex, only to run the other way as soon as he or she falls in love with you? Is fighting with your spouse or lover necessary for you to have a satisfying sexual experience? Do you feel compelled to have sexual affairs in order to prevent closeness?

Sometimes difficulties with your children will illustrate your problems with relationships. You have probably noticed that in some families intense conflicts develop that seem impossible to resolve. In spite of anger and punishment from their parents, for example, some children continue to behave provocatively with a particular parent or sibling.

Usually we assume that people are simply too lazy to do anything about their problems, but perhaps that is because it's too unpleasant to think that there are some things we just can't change. Think of all the New Year's resolutions you have broken! Why can't you do anything about the things you hate in your life?

It seems logical that self-interest would be sufficient to motivate us to change those things about ourselves that we dislike or that get us into trouble. In fact, most people assume or have been taught that a person's behavior results from a desire for positive feedback from others and the wish to avoid negative experience. If seeking pleasure and avoiding pain are so crucial in motivating behavior, why don't people avoid painful and self-destructive patterns and pursue what is fulfilling, instead of continuing to behave in ways they hate?

You probably consider yourself a rational, clear-thinking person who knows how to make good decisions in most aspects of your life. You may be particularly frustrated if you enjoy success in some areas but not others. Are you just a failure in these areas? Or is it possible that some factor unknown to you is contributing to your problem? Does the answer somehow remain just beyond the grasp of your understanding?

Your outward problem is evident to you. If you were asked, "What one area do you really struggle with?" you would have an answer. Your trouble is obvious. It is like the tip of a threatening iceberg jutting above a quiet sea.

What is unclear is what's beneath the surface. How big is the obstacle and of what configuration? Can you learn to sail past it, or will you be destroyed by continually crashing into this hidden barrier? Most frustrating of all is the certain knowledge that you are the one who is causing the collisions. But since the origin of your problem is not visible, you can't avoid it.

People want to be successful and happy in life and not feel compelled to do things that work against their aspirations and values. Are you accomplishing your goals? Or are you instead acting in self-defeating ways in spite of your best intentions and efforts?

You may have read self-help books. Did they work? Why are you reading this one? Maybe you're reading it for the same reason I wrote it: because many other books don't get to the source of your problem.

If you find yourself behaving in ways you hate, getting bad reactions from those around you, and having little success using willpower to change your actions, something beyond your control is dictating those actions. In my years of clinical experience and research I've seen that when people uncover their hidden mind-sets, they can change what they're dissatisfied with.

Once people see what lies beneath the surface, similar to the truly destructive part of the iceberg, they can sail past the surface problem successfully.

What is it that interferes with your ability to change what you hate? What is beneath the surface?

Corrupting Mind-Sets: The Computer Virus of Your Mind

Years ago computer specialists became aware of an "illness" in their electronic servants. Computer viruses, introduced by some outside contamination, were causing computers to respond improperly. Commands were ignored through the effects of over-riding but hidden countermeasures.

Sound familiar?

We all have an internal system of behavioral control that I call mind-sets. They are like the operational system of a computer, which controls day-to-day functions automatically. Included are ideas, values, and rules that have become ingrained over the course of our lives, mainly in response to our parents and siblings. These thought patterns enable us to make choices and to achieve goals. They incorporate our foundational beliefs about ourselves and other people, what we expect from others, and how we respond to others. Included in these beliefs are our interpretations of the behavior of others, good and bad, right and wrong.

Like the hidden pathways of a computer, mind-sets exist in our unconscious mind: the part of our mind that contains thoughts, feelings, and impressions of which we are unaware. Because of this, they are difficult to access and understand and, therefore, are inaccessible to change.

Your mind-sets developed side by side with your conscious thinking during your childhood. When you learned childhood rules like "Raise your hand before you speak in class," at first you had to make an effort to remember them. Eventually it became second nature. Now, though you no longer need some of those rules, they are still part of your unconscious mind.

Over time your childhood beliefs became ingrained, whether they were true or not. You can see how this could cause you to have problems later on. Your mind-sets are your personal rules for life, which are buried within your unconscious and rule your reactions with the power of ethical and religious doctrine. Many of them are reasonable and don't cause you to suffer.

But what about unreasonable thoughts, ideas, and rules that run your life and make no sense in view of their negative effects on you? What are the hidden codes of instruction that make you act, think, and feel in ways you despise? What is the logic behind inner rules that were adaptive for you as a child because of the problems within your family? How were they formed, and why do they remain in your current life? What are the responses they cause in you? And what happens when, like a computer with a virus, your mind-sets are counterproductive to your true goals?

The mind-sets we are going to focus on are those that compel you to behave in ways you hate. They are the ones that developed in relation to the major defects of your parents and siblings and have become like destructive computer viruses.

Destructive mind-sets result from the unusual and incorrect ideas and conclusions you arrive at regarding your parents' and siblings' serious flaws, neglect, and harmful and abusive attitudes. Your conclusions about these negative characteristics and behavior take the form of mental rules that become more and more firmly set over time. As we will see, these mental rules are held in place by guilt. The responses you make to these mind-sets are ruinous to your well-being and cause you to keep behaving in ways you hate throughout your life in spite of the self-destructive effects of such behavior. In other words, you feel guilty about doing what is in your best interests.

As a child you are new to the game of life. Your lack of previous experience with people makes it difficult for you to decide whether you or your parents or your siblings are responsible for what goes wrong. A primitive tribe facing natural disasters blames itself for earthquakes, floods, droughts, and so on, saying, "We've angered the gods." Similarly, as a child, you blame yourself for unpleasant experiences that are not your fault. Blaming yourself has a purpose, and you will learn what it is. But this self-blame is the major cause of the behaviors that plague you.

By contrast, as an adult you have a pretty good idea whether someone else's behavior is their personal problem or is related to you. For example, as an adult if you meet someone who acts badly because he or she is a jerk, you don't assume it is your fault. You know that the behavior has nothing to do with you, and therefore doesn't require you to apologize or bend over backwards to please him or her at your expense.

If you could enter a time machine and be reborn into your original family, except that this time around you would retain all of the knowledge you have acquired as an adult, wouldn't your life turn out differently? You bet it would. When your parents or siblings consistently behaved badly, you would know that it had nothing to do with you. Therefore, you would be no more affected by them than you would by some jerk you met at a cocktail party. You wouldn't need to change your normal behavior, and you could grow up to fulfill all of your potential.

Destructive mind-sets cause you to feel guilty, just as you do when you violate an ingrained ethical or religious doctrine. This guilt is painful, and like a wrestler's forceful armhold, it will make you submit. The problem is that certain mind-sets compel you to behave in ways you hate.

I will discuss this cycle in depth in the following chapters of this book, but here it is in a nutshell: Many of us hold to sets of destructive beliefs that were developed in our unconscious mind in childhood. Although these beliefs cause us to feel and behave self-destructively, attempting to disobey or overcome them in order to pursue our normal goals causes us to experience strong feelings of guilt. Conversely, when we obey, we often find ourselves acting in ways that are hurtful to our life and well-being. This causes deep resentment in us, which leads to rebellion and other self-defeating behavior. Finally, impossible as it seems, we can be forced against our will to adopt the very qualities of our parents that we hated.

You may not believe that you could be controlled this way, but if you find yourself behaving in ways you hate and are unable to change, you are probably acting according to a corrupting mind-set. Like a computer virus that commands misinformation and often causes a computer to act self-destructively, these "self-viruses" interfere with your goals and fulfillment and cause you to act self-destructively, too.

Always Be Nice to Others: Good or Bad?

Let's take as an example the mind-set "Always be nice to others." We'll get back to how this rule might be formed, but for now let's look at how it may affect you in adult life. "Always be nice to others" sounds like a great mind-set to have. On the surface it has a positive moral value for those who hold it. But for the person who suffers from excessive guilt about breaking this rule, it becomes a trap. Most people are able to choose to be nice when it's appropriate and to refuse when it's ruinous to their well-being.

If you aren't able to oppose the mind-set "Always be nice to others," you'll become a slave to this rule. Can you see how slavishly obeying this rule might cause people to become doormats? At the same time, such people might hate always giving in to others and not understand why they can't change. Some people feel good while they are performing acts of self-sacrifice, but may end up feeling that they have been exploited or not taken seriously.

How Destructive Mind-Sets Work

So now we know the enemy's name. But how does this "computer virus" infect our mind? And how does it work on us?

We will discuss these and other important points in the chapters that follow:

- **Hidden Enemies.** It's hard to do battle with a hidden enemy. Why are our mind-sets so hard to uncover, when recognizing them is essential to our well being?
- **Primitive Thinking.** Like a primitive tribe that thinks it is at fault for the calamities of nature that befall it, we tend to blame our-selves for our parents' and siblings' mistakes and faults. This irrational self-blame is one of the crucial factors in creating the behavior, thoughts, and feelings we hate.
- **Good Morals.** In addition to the Ten Commandments, we have all developed our own subjective set of moral commandments and values that appear to have validity and merit, but in fact can chain us to behavior and thoughts we hate.
- **Bent Twigs.** The adage, "As the twig is bent so grows the tree" really applies here. Behavior we hate (which often causes unwanted reactions from others) originates in childhood but continues into adult life. Why does such behavior persist when it is damaging to our well-being? If we are no longer under the influence of the parents and/or siblings who caused our misconceptions, why are we still captured by these mind-sets?
- **Self–Trash Talk.** Like a plague, we can be tortured by thoughts that we hate, such as "I'm no good," "I'm selfish," "I'm lazy," "I'm rotten," "I'm stupid," and so on and be unable to free ourselves of them. We will discuss how and why this takes place.
- **Accommodation.** To maintain the important ties to our parents or siblings, we may accommodate to or comply with their serious defects and damaging expectations, and in the process ignore our own interests, goals, and destiny. For example, you might become extremely obedient to a very overbearing and controlling parent and as a result squelch your ability to think independently. Not only will this compliance very likely cause you to suffer in profound ways, but the deep and bitter resent-

ment that you endure, even if it is suppressed, can exert a powerful negative force on your life. We will discuss why accommodation is so difficult to resist.

- **Rebellion.** Quiet or open rebellion, defiance as a protest against parental oppression, deficiencies, and strangeness can cause severe self-destructive behavior and guilt feelings. There is no escape from the damaging effects of harsh and painful guilt feelings. For example, if you rebelliously defy an overbearing parent by stubbornly acting contrary to their expectations, you may feel very guilty for provoking him or her. Guilt feelings will make you pay, and we will explore how.

- **Mimicry.** As adults we often mimic the harmful behavior of our parents and siblings in spite of vowing to be different and better than they when we grow up. I call this "doing to your children and others what was done to you." You may swear to yourself that you will be different, but you will likely be unable to escape copying the same behavior patterns. We will discuss why this comes about and what the consequences are.

The purpose of this book is to help you to understand how and why as a child you responded to your flawed parents and siblings with self-defeating behavior, feelings, and thoughts, and why they continue throughout your whole life. At any time, feel free to view the charts in the back of the book, which will provide you with quick insight into the sources of your self-defeating behaviors, and which of your specific hidden beliefs and feelings are responsible for the behaviors you hate. You will also learn how to use this information to change what you dislike about yourself. To do so, in Chapter Eleven, I have made it possible for you to create personality profiles of everyone in your family by answering six questions, so that you can quickly discover the most damaging qualities of your parents and siblings. As they become clearer, the charts will become more useful too.

CHAPTER TWO

Stuck!

TO BEGIN, LET'S EXAMINE HOW destructive thoughts and feelings become set in our minds with the strength of moral laws. This is important, because right or wrong, helpful or self-destructive, our mind-sets are firmly stuck in our unconscious. And the glue that holds them in place is guilt.

Guilt: The Glue of Destructive Mind-Sets

How would you have felt if, as a child, you received an electric shock every time you acted in your own behalf? Suppose this happened every time you spoke up for yourself? Eventually, even though saying what you thought was important for your sense of well being, you would stop doing it. In effect, this is how guilt feelings affect your behavior. They act like an electric shock that restrains many of your normal behaviors. The electric shock signals to you that this action is wrong and it is your fault.

Remember, as adults we know that when someone acts inappropriately it is the result of his or her personal problem, and that it is not related to us. But it's different for children.

As a child, your lack of previous experience in life made it difficult for you to decide whether you or your parent or sibling was responsible when they acted inappropriately. You were susceptible to blaming yourself for all that went wrong. You didn't have the knowledge to think, "I wonder what's wrong with him," or "She must have had a bad day," or "He is depressed because his business is not doing well." Instead, you blamed yourself for events that were not your fault and changed your normal behavior.

Why, as a child would you do this? If you make yourself responsible as a child for what goes wrong, you hope that by changing your behavior you can make things right. Like a primitive tribe, you are still trying to appease your parents, the gods of your childhood.

Let's say that one of your parents regularly screamed in an out-of-control way because you weren't obedient and submissive enough. If you lacked the perspective that your parent had a lifelong personality problem, you might easily blame yourself and feel guilty for causing him or her to act out of control. To avoid experiencing this strong feeling of self-blame, you would most likely become overly obedient, and then hate yourself for it.

Every time you, as a child, were caused by guilt feelings to put aside your healthy goals in order to comply with the flaws of your parents or siblings, you were forced into acting self-destructively. If this persisted over a long period of time, it became fixed as an automatic pattern: a mind-set.

Why Do I Feel Guilty?

Guilt is activated by our behavior, thoughts, or feelings that we judge to be wrong or bad. It means that we believe that something we are doing is causing pain to someone else. It doesn't matter that your behavior is normal. If it is associated with a parent or sibling consistently acting badly for a long time, you will feel at fault.

Normal parents are protective of their children. What if your parents were overprotective? What if every time you played sports, rode your bike, or roughhoused with your friends, your parents became disturbed and frantic? "Watch out, you'll get hurt," they might say, or "You're ruining my life." Would you have interpreted that as true interest? You probably would have believed that your parents were being hurt by your sense of adventure and fun. Children who think that their actions are causing pain for their parents will feel guilt.

Let's be clear. We're not talking about a normal range of caution and concern, but a hyper range: extreme caution and worry over small risks. A man or woman who has grown up under this kind of guilt will also experience guilt in response to taking risks as an adult. You will still feel that you are offending them.

If this applies to you, you may not even be aware that you feel guilty, but the guilt feeling will operate like a subtle shock. It's similar to the jolt a dog receives from an electric collar every time it reaches a certain boundary. The guilt will increase in intensity the closer you approach forbidden acts, thoughts, or feelings. Your sense of guilt, whether overt or subconscious, is a warning that you are trespassing in an area you should be avoiding.

Religious people are often conscious of sinful thoughts or deeds that make them experience guilt. Early training in a specific system of belief establishes mind-sets pertaining to that system. But in this case the rules are visible and the guilt is therefore reasonable. Feeling guilty about stealing something, for example, when you have been taught that stealing is wrong, is a logical response.

But what confusion can result from the guilt that arises when trying to do something good for yourself, you violate a corrupting mind-set. When you try to lose weight, be adventurous, get good grades, become independent, or reject a request for money in opposition to your childhood mind-sets, you may feel the same as someone who is violating a religious commandment. And yet you don't know why! You probably won't be aware that it is happening. Your guilt is a signal that you have violated the command of a mind-set.

As a Child You Think Like a Primitive Tribe

As a child you react to the world around you like a primitive tribe experiencing a natural disaster:

Deep within the rain forest a small tribe of men, women and children danced with abandon around the edge of a large fire pit. Their fertility celebration took place at the base of a great basaltic mountain. Now they would be allowed to marry and bring forth more children!

Suddenly joy turned to terror as the rumbling and rolling of the earth warned that the mountain was active. The leaders of the tribe quickly gathered before the hut of the wise man. His advanced age showed his ability to survive. All grew quiet as the old one began to speak.

His voice was frail and thin, but his clear eyes drew the people's attention away from the clouds of smoke now rising from the mountain. "Hear me," he said. "The mountain fire god is angry at your celebration. Stop your singing and dancing. You have disturbed his sleep. Go quietly to your homes and pray that he will again become drowsy."

Obediently, the crowd dispersed as the wise man said.

Two young warriors walked sullenly back to their father's tent. The older of the two spoke under his breath to his brother: "Now I must spend another year in Father's tent and not marry, all because of the fire god."

This tribe is in the same situation that you were in as a child: It has insufficient knowledge of the causes of the disaster it experiences, and as a result is helpless to do anything about it. Like a child, the only variable the tribe has control over is its own behavior. In order to solve its sense of helplessness, the tribe assumes that its behavior has angered the gods of nature.

The tribe, therefore, hopes that by altering its behavior through praying, performing rituals, and inhibiting or changing specific actions, it can placate the gods and thereby alleviate the natural disaster.

But by altering its behavior in the attempt to make things work out, the tribe may have made compromises that are detrimental to its well being. In the above story the warrior has to postpone having a family. Other edicts from the wise man might command that the tribe make other changes that are harmful to the group.

Similarly, as a child you assumed that your behavior was responsible for provoking your parents. This assumption was often simply a general feeling and not clearly thought out. But it was based on real experience with siblings or parents who were continually hurt, threatened, jealous, or angered by one of your normal behaviors. In response to this, you probably changed or inhibited your actions or attitudes in order to not hurt them, hoping to get your parents to change the behavior that was detrimental to you. In other words, you changed something normal in yourself in order to not hurt someone else.

When your parents or siblings acted hurt by you, you were experiencing them fairly accurately, and not making it up. They showed it by shouting, rejecting, pouting, withdrawing, and sulking. They clearly said it by saying things like "How could you do this to me?," "You are ruining my life," "I had a nervous breakdown because of you," "I hope your children do to you what you have done to me," and so on.

You struggled to behave in ways that would appease your parents—just as the tribe tried to appease the gods—even if trying to appease them meant compromising or inhibiting important normal goals for yourself. How you did this will be explained in detail.

We all want to control what is unpleasant and damaging to us. If your parents were overtly abusive, an outside observer would likely assume that your reason for conforming to your parents' bad behavior was to avoid continually being hurt by them (negative reinforcement). But when a parent is overpossessive, overprotective, needy, controlling, rejecting, and so on, the reason for a child's response to their behavior is not so obvious. As a child, you truly believed that you were hurting your parents every time they were provoked by your behavior.

After all, you did see them become upset, violent, rejecting, depressed, withdrawn, intoxicated, competitive, burdened, needy, and so on in response to something you normally did, just as the primitive tribe heard the rumbling of the volcano. Therefore, like the tribe, you became highly motivated to stop doing what you thought was disturbing your parents, because you needed them so much.

Here's another example of the same pattern: Let's imagine that you are hired by a firm that you know nothing about. Further, let's say that the job is essential to you. Your livelihood depends on keeping this job. However, you have been given no knowledge about the staff and the boss, and you have been given no information about your job.

You notice that your boss acts in ways that are rejecting towards you. What are you to think? You have no previous experience with your boss, and therefore little ability to make judgments about him. You also have no knowledge of what is expected of you in order to perform your job. Therefore, it will be extremely difficult for you to decide whether your boss's attitude toward you is the result of your performance on the job or of his personality.

You can see the parallels between the situation of the tribe, the employee, and you as a young child. *In all three examples, the lack of previous experience and knowledge limits the ability to draw proper connections between cause and effect.*

As an employee who was suffering rejection, you would probably feel compelled to search for something in your own behavior in order to explain the unpleasant rejecting attitude of your boss. You would probably examine everything you had done, hoping to discover the cause of his rejection, in order to spare yourself the grief being inflicted on you.

Like the primitive tribe, you might decide that something in your behavior or attitude is responsible for your boss's rejection of you, and then you would attempt to modify it in order to prevent future rejection.

Your conclusions about what you were doing that was responsible for your boss's rejecting behavior would determine the content of your mind-set. If you assume that his rejection of you was because you were independent, outspoken, or unassertive, for example, you would be inclined to stop those behaviors. This is a crucial concept because, remember, that mind-set would then guide your future actions. And your guilt would cement your mind-set into place. Why? *It is what you believe hurts your parents (or your boss or the gods) that causes you to block a specific behavior or sacrifice an important goal for yourself.*

Let's look at three examples to clarify what destructive mind-sets are like and how the self-defeating behaviors they cause are kept firmly in place by guilt. The three women you are about to meet had different mind-sets, yet shared similar problems with weight. It's helpful to see how their mind-sets were formed and how they responded to them. These examples of childhood thinking follow the logic of the primitive tribe.

Meet Mary, Pat, and Alice

MARY

A grossly overweight client named Mary had the thought, "If I'm beautiful and admired by my father, it will cause my mother to feel jealous and hurt." The product of a dysfunctional family, she was appreciated by her father, who was indifferent to her mother. Understandably, Mary's mother was greatly distressed by her husband's lack of attention to her.

As a child Mary believed that her father's appreciation of her was responsible for his lack of attention to her mother. She thought it was her fault that her mother was unhappy. Guilt over supposedly harming her mother by being attractive reinforced the thought, which developed into the mind-set "Being fat and unattractive is good."

Although Mary was unaware of this mind-set, it operated to cause the overweight pattern she hated in herself as an adult. Her deep-seated belief undermined every attempt to lose weight.

Each time she dieted, hidden guilt caused her to gain the unwanted pounds back. She unconsciously worried about making her mother—and by extension all women—feel envious of her attractiveness to men.

Furthermore, Mary's problem grew in intensity. The closer she got to her goal of being beautiful, the more guilty she felt. Controlled by the mind-set "Being fat and unattractive is good (because Mom isn't harmed)," Mary remained unable to do what was necessary to be appealing to men as an accommodation to her mother's plight.

Let's look more closely at Mary's conclusions. What would you think, as an adult, if one of your parents told you they were divorcing the other because you were more attractive? Wouldn't you think that was absurd? Is it likely that you would accept blame for your parent's fault?

But when Mary was a child she made an incorrect connection between cause and effect. She blamed herself for her mother's unhappiness with her father, even though her parents' difficulties were independent of her (their problems preceded her birth). She did this in order to try to protect her mother. This was a destructive mind-set.

PAT

In another example, a married woman named Pat came to see me with complaints about her eating habits, which involved bingeing and starving herself. Pat's siblings had similar difficulties. How did they develop?

Her father's eating habits were normal, but her mother's habits with food alternated between binge eating and starving herself. Also, her mother's habits with money alternated between stinginess and compulsive shopping. Why did my client follow her mother's eating habits and not her father's?

Her mother's main satisfactions derived from overinvolvement in the decisions and life of her children. Guilt made it difficult for them to become independent of her. Pat erroneously assumed that her mother's anguish over food and money was caused by Pat's desire to become independent of her.

As a result, Pat developed the thought "If I become independent and make my own decisions, my mother will feel that her life is diminished. That will cause her to either binge or starve, and become tight with money or overspend."

The mind-set that developed from this thought was "Independence is bad." In response to this mind-set, my client prevented herself from identifying with her father's attitudes about food and money and instead modeled herself after her mother.

How did this mechanism of identification work? Pat irrationally believed that by attempting to become independent she caused her mother's eating problems. She felt guilty for hurting her mother in this way.

This, in turn, made her feel that she deserved to have the same eating problems she had caused her mother to have (atonement). Therefore, Pat became like her mother rather than eating in a normal way like her father. In addition, her eating habits were a way for Pat to reassure her mother that Pat was like her and not independent of her.

Let's look more closely at Pat's conclusions. What would you think, as an adult, if your mother told you that she was both extravagant and stingy with money and food because you were making independent decisions? Wouldn't you think that was absurd? Is it likely that you would accept blame for these problems?

But as a child with limited experience, that is exactly what Pat inferred from her mother's problems. Like Mary, she accepted blame and responsibility and acted to try to alleviate the effects of her perceived misdeeds.

Mary's self-destructive message caused her to avoid being attractive to men. Her guilt feeling resulted from her thinking, "I hurt women by making them envious." Pat's self-destructive message caused her to alternate between binge eating and starving herself. Her guilt feeling resulted from thinking that "I hurt my mother by being independent of her or by being more like my father." Both of these women acted automatically and self-destructively because of destructive mind-sets.

Have you come to false conclusions about your own experiences? Have you concluded that you are responsible for the faults and problems of others and that as a result you have to pay?

If we apply the principles of positive and negative reinforcement to Mary's case, we will see a great irony. The negative outcome (being overweight) was not the result of negative reinforcement, but came about because of her father's appreciation. And paradoxically, the positive outcome (looking attractive) eluded her in spite of positive reinforcement (again, her father's appreciation). Because of a hidden mind-set (reinforced by guilt toward her mother), Mary incorrectly believed that she was the cause of her mother's plight.

ALICE

Alice, another overweight client of mine, was required by her upper-class parents to rigidly obey their social standards and was strongly reprimanded if she didn't. She was expected to have proper social graces, play only with children of their class, adhere to their political outlook, and be athletic, trim, and beautiful. The source of her weight problem was different from Mary's or Pat's.

As a child, Alice worried that her parents would feel betrayed and hurt if she made her own choices in life. This kept her from becoming aware of how deeply resentful she felt about being so strongly controlled by them. As a result, she was the perfect child. Her destructive mind-set was "Thinking for myself is a crime because my parents will feel diminished."

When Alice got older she increasingly rebelled against their control over her in order to relieve her resentment about not having a life of her own. To prove to herself that she had a separate identity, she began to follow her own rules. She stopped playing sports, became heavy, dressed poorly, adopted contrary political views, and socialized with people who would have offended her parents.

Alice never actually developed her own independent ideas and values. Her hidden mind-set required her to strictly adhere to her parents' views or to those opposite to them. Overeating was part of the rebelliousness necessary to maintain her sense of uniqueness. She couldn't achieve her conscious goal to be healthy and trim because it coincided with her parents' outlook. Meeting their standard for looks made her feel that she didn't have a mind of her own. She said, "It makes me feel like a nothing."

As an adult, if your parents said their life was ruined because you were not exactly like them, would you accept blame?

There are three other common causes of continually overeating. One is a result of overeating as a rebellion against parents who withhold food, particularly desserts, either as a punishment or because they are excessively worried about their child's weight. The resentment that these children feel about being deprived or cheated is expressed by rebelliously sneaking and hiding food, especially desserts. Alice did it to rebel against having to be perfect.

The second motivation for overeating is to please parents who mainly feel fulfilled from feeding their children. As a result, these children are reluctant to stop eating when full because they feel guilty about disappointing their parents' need for happiness.

The third is based on feeling sorry for an obese parent or sibling. If you have control over your weight, and that makes you feel that you are better off, your sense of guilt may cause you to also lose control over your eating habits. Or if you are like Pat, and think that your behavior is responsible for a parent being fat, you may have to pay yourself back (punishment) by also becoming fat.

If Mary, Pat, or Alice had tried to lose weight by following the advice of a self-help book or by willpower, would they have succeeded? Could they have overcome their hidden mind-sets and underlying destructive feelings of guilt or rebellion? Without understanding these underlying beliefs (which have religious authority), they would probably have had great difficulty changing their behavior. As soon as they progressed toward losing weight, feelings of either guilt or rebellion would intensify and divert them from their goal.

However, they all made progress once they learned about the beliefs that were behind their actions. They began to understand that they were behaving according to incorrect conclusions they had made as children about experiences in their families. This gave them greater control over the feelings of guilt or rebellion that were making them behave in ways they hated, and that enabled them to succeed.

It's interesting to see what happened in these women's lives. And it's helpful to understand the hidden mind-sets that caused the weight problem they despised. But naturally, the question comes to mind: How did the situation come about in the first place? Let's take a look at mismatches between parents and children.

CHAPTER THREE

Left Shoe, Right Foot: When Your Parent Doesn't Fit

Have you ever had a blind date with someone that turned out to be a painful mismatch? Imagine yourself in the following situation (male and female roles can of course be reversed):

You squint slightly as you look for the number on the mailbox. *Yes, there it is, Apartment 13. What was it she said? Up the stairs, and it's the last door on the left. She had such a pleasant voice! Of course, that was her roommate. But surely someone with a nice roommate would be nice as well,* you reason.

The flowers you bought at the grocery store look cheerful. *I'm glad I stopped,* you think, *even if it did make me a few minutes late.* Stepping up to the door, you smartly ring the bell. You start as the door is jerked open from the other side. Here she is, your date. The pleasant smile freezes on your face.

The first thing you notice is her lipstick. It's a dark maroon color and is painted carefully past the edges of her thin lips to make them look larger. Her blue eyes are ringed, top and bottom, with sky blue eye shadow.

She shoves a hand into yours and begins pumping as if you need priming, saying "I'm June, and you're . . ." You begin to answer, but she continues:

"...late!"

"I got these for you," you try to recover with a smile.

"They look like they came from the grocery store," she says. "Nice, though they don't last as long as flowers from a real florist. Where are we going to dinner?"

"I thought we'd try the new Mexican restaurant near the theater," you answer.

"That sounds good," she says. Then she proceeds to tell you all about the problems she has with flatulence after she eats beans.

This inauspicious beginning to your evening merely foreshadows the depths of despair you'll endure all night long.

Have you ever been trapped in such an evening? Do you remember the squeamish, gut-wrenching feeling that overtook you as you anticipated the agony of spending an evening with someone you couldn't stand? Do you remember scheming to get out of it as quickly as possible, and vowing to never go on a blind date again unless you were assured in advance that the next one would be absolutely perfect? I'm certain that you, like most people in this situation, were determined to forget the experience as quickly as possible.

Now imagine that you bring "June" home at the end of the evening. She turns at the door and hands you the key. Obligingly, you insert it into the lock and step back slightly as the door swings inward. She looks at you questioningly. *Oh*, you think, *I need to be careful what I say here. The last thing I want is a repeat performance!* "Well, June, it's been a lovely evening," you say and extend your hand politely.

She grimaces, "What are you doing? When did we start shaking hands? Kinda formal for married people."

"Married?" you stammer, horrified.

"Of course, married. I've been your wife for two years. Forty-eight more to go." She cackles, and you notice the maroon lipstick has crept into the lines around her lips. Suddenly you realize—she's right! You only dreamed this was a blind date! You are married!

This horrific "blind date" without any recourse or possibility of escape should give you a sense of the problem facing children who have painful mismatches with their parents.

When we discuss painful or traumatic experiences that children can have as a result of mismatches with parents or siblings, think of this date and multiply the emotional distress tenfold, and that will help you to understand why we repress memories of situations that were painful for us as children. Just as we try to forget an unpleasant blind date, we try to forget painful childhood memories.

It may seem very obvious and overly simplistic to say that we needed our parents in order to survive, but it is because of this fundamental fact of life that you may have been one of those unfortunate children who had to adapt to parents who were peculiar, cruel, rejecting, self-centered, envious, competitive, needy, depressed, drug-dependent, possessive, controlling, overly enamored of you, and so on.

Learning to accommodate to consistently neurotic behavior or maltreatment in childhood causes us to be self-destructive as adults. The mind-sets that arise out of these experiences and your responses to them are responsible for the behavior that you despise. As a child, you incorrectly blamed yourself for what was unpleasant and changed your behavior to make things better. But in changing your behavior to get along with your parents, you compromised important goals for yourself. Blaming yourself for their faults established your guilt. If you were guilty, you had to pay. One way that you may have paid was by mimicking the bad behavior of your parents, taking on the very qualities you believed you caused them to have.

Mismatched

You and your parents have a powerful biological and emotional investment in each other and naturally want things to work out between you. As a child, you needed your parents and they needed you. In an average family, where the personalities of the parents are fairly reasonable over time and the child's innate qualities are not extreme, serious conflicts usually do not occur.

However, ongoing problems arise when serious mismatches between the personalities of children and parents persist over a long period of time, resulting in a prolonged conflict of interests. When mistreatment, deficiency, and weakness in their parents remain constant for many years, children are not able to discount the behavior of the parents as an aberration or a minor problem. Children want to believe that their parents don't really mean to mistreat them, and for the most part, they don't: Their actions are simply uncontrolled reflexes caused by the mind-sets they developed in dealing with their own parents. Children desperately want to convince themselves of the goodness of their parents, because their well being depends on it and because they have no control over the parents' behavior.

The only variable children can control is their own behavior. If you, as a child, blamed yourself for your parents' displeasure and changed your behavior, you hoped your parents would act more positively. If you thought you were at fault for your parents' mistreatment, you felt guilt and thought you had to atone for it.

If you decided that your parents weren't really flawed, then you could bypass the whole issue. *That is why you may still deny much of what you see in your parents and give them better grades than they deserve. By seeing them in a good light, you don't have to blame yourself for what went wrong.* If, in your mind, less of what takes place is your fault, you won't feel so obligated to hold back doing what is good for you. If there's no debt, you don't have to pay.

The Price You Pay When Mismatched with Your Parents

So far we've looked at mind-sets and how they develop. We've seen that they can be hidden and that they are cemented into position by deep feelings of guilt. Moreover, we've seen examples of people who hated their behavior, yet who couldn't change without understanding their mind-sets. But their problems were different. The guilt feelings didn't always produce the same responses.

What are the different ways children respond when problems arise in their families?

Children will often accommodate to their parents' needs and suppress their own needs, even when their parents act badly. Sometimes, they will rebel and protest against their parents' flaws. Amazingly, they may also blame themselves for their parents' faults and mimic the very behavior they hate in their parents.

Let's look at each of these responses more closely.

ACCOMMODATION

This is how Mary (Chapter Two) responded to the problems in her family. Mary accommodated to her mother's unhappiness in a particular way. In response to the family circumstances of her father paying more attention to Mary, but acting indifferently to her mother and her mother's subsequent suffering, Mary falsely took the blame. She assumed that her attractiveness was responsible for her father's interest in her, causing her mother's plight. By developing the mind-set "Being fat and unattractive is good," she hoped to spare her mother from suffering.

Children accommodate to their parents' faults in order to not hurt them, and to feel loved by them. This relieves their sense of having hurt their parents by not living up to their expectations. However, in the process of accommodating, they can compromise important goals.

Imagine that, as a child, you had an overprotective mother who became agitated every time you moved out of her sight. In response you might have developed the thought "I'd better not be too adventurous, because it's agitating and hurting my mother." That thought could have eventually created the mind-set "Caution is best."

Following this unconscious rule in all aspects of your life, you could easily have inhibited your innate spontaneity, sense of adventure, and sports, something you might have deeply resented. However, not being cautious will make you feel guilty for causing your mother to suffer.

If you continued to follow this mind-set in your adult life, you would probably hate yourself for being too cautious and restricted, and would be continually baffled as to why you behaved in this particular way. Or, if you were comfortable with your cautious style, it might cause others to become frustrated and irritated with you. In either case you might never realize that you are simply paying for your guilt towards your mother.

Let's review how this works: If your parents were overly worried about you getting hurt and as a result acted overprotective towards you, you would feel responsible for making them frantic and thereby hurting them by playing sports and being adventurous. Being yourself caused your parents pain.

If you had decided to participate in sports, they would have felt distressed by it because you could have been hurt. If you had decided to avoid athletics to relieve your parents' anxiety, you would have inhibited something important to you. Additionally, you would probably have deeply resented your parents' overprotectiveness for interfering with your healthy development and limiting your athletic interests and sense of adventure.

In another case, if your mother needed involvement with you and was always upset when you pursued your interests without her or pursued relationships with others, you could have stopped hurting her by staying tied to her apron strings. In this way, by accommodating to her possessiveness, you would have held yourself back from relationships with others, which would have been detrimental to you.

If your parents were very authoritarian and controlling, it would also have been self-destructive if you had become too submissive, obedient, or restricted thinking for yourself.

Accommodating yourself to your parents' (and your siblings') flawed behavior interferes with your healthy development, but if you don't accommodate to them you feel guilty for hurting them by behaving in ways that are normal and good for you.

This is what reinforces mind-sets. If you try to do something that makes you feel good, you experience guilt because you connect it with hurting someone else. Therefore, you feel like a sinner who must pay. Because these self-defeating ideas are usually hidden from your conscious awareness, it is very difficult to change the behaviors you hate. This book will help you to become consciously aware of your hidden self-defeating motivations so that you can change them.

Remember the pain you felt with a mismatched blind date? Thankfully, this only lasts a short time. Contrast this with your childhood predicament, where you are stuck with your parents and siblings for years, no matter what. Think of the accumulated resentment that builds up after years of accommodating to behaviors you know that aren't right for you.

To relieve your sense of frustration and resentment about being a slave to your parents' and siblings' exaggerated requirements, you may offset your exasperation by rebelling and protesting instead of accommodating.

REBELLION

Most people know what rebellion is. We use the term here to describe a child's refusal to comply with parental demands or needs, and the restrictions they impose. We rebel against accommodating to our parents in order to fight their unconscious or overt attempts to negatively limit our development.

Children are usually unable to complain to their parents about how their parents' specific behavior is spoiling their life. Therefore, rebellion as a protest is meant to signal parents that their actions are distressing and ought to stop. Unfortunately, because parents have their own hidden mind-sets, they don't get the correct message but instead become even more provoked by their children's rebellious protests. Therefore the cycle of parent-child conflict continues unchanged.

There is some relief in not going along with what parents demand, because children then feel that they are protecting their own values and interests. However, by not doing what their parents expect, children will feel guilty about hurting them. In addition, rebellion may cause children to behave in self-destructive ways. Rebellious attitudes often spoil our effectiveness with others because people experience us as uncooperative, provocative, and uninterested.

Children can permanently stay rebellious (Alice), or they may alternate that position with accommodation. When the guilt of defiance and protest accumulates because children have thwarted what their parents' want, they usually shift back to the more accommodating position that they resent, beginning the cycle again.

Thus, children rebel to avoid the restrictions caused by accommodation, then suffer so much guilt for their rebellion that they accommodate to find relief from it. The end result is that they simply shift back and forth between the two evils and never find true relief (excessive accommodation causing resentment and excessive rebellion causing guilt). You may notice these opposite swings in your own behavior.

If your father was domineering, for example, you might have become stubborn, rigid, and defiant in order to protect yourself from being dominated. Did you want to be stubborn, rigid, and defiant? No, but neither did you want to be dominated. Your rebellion produced traits that you may still hate but can't change without recognizing their source.

Imagine that as a child with overprotective parents you became a daredevil to protest against your parents' restrictiveness. Your new mind-set would have been "Throw caution to the wind." You can see how this commandment could have driven you to become wildly adventurous to the point of danger.

If you were lucky enough to not be injured or killed, you would still have suffered guilt from unnerving and frightening your overprotective parents. You would hate yourself for still feeling driven to the edge of danger, without understanding the cause.

DOING TO OTHERS WHAT WAS DONE TO YOU (MIMICKING)

The third response you might have made when faced with conflict in your family was to do to others what was done to you, thereby mimicking your parent. This may seem incredible. Why would you have done this, especially after vowing that when you grew up you would be different and better?

There are several reasons.

The first reason we become like our parents is to punish ourselves and relieve our guilt for hurting them. If you think you are responsible for causing your parents' faults, then you deserve to be punished by having the same faults. Just as a primitive tribe blames itself for acts of nature, a child blames itself when a parent is bad. For example, if as a child you think that by being smart you make your father feel inadequate, you might also feel that you have to be inadequate yourself to atone for your father's feelings of inadequacy; in other words, being like him keeps you from being better than him. This is the price you pay for making him feel inadequate.

If you blame yourself for your mother's overprotectiveness, you might punish yourself by becoming overprotective toward your own children and others. You now suffer from excessive worry when your children are active in sports, thereby paying yourself back for the suffering you felt responsible for causing your parents to feel. If you blame yourself for your father's domineering behavior, you might punish yourself by becoming domineering. This is self-destructive, because you would probably prefer not to act domineering toward your children, and then have to suffer from their accommodating and rebellious behavior towards you.

The idea is that if you caused your parents or siblings to suffer, then you deserve to suffer in the same way. This principle, the dynamic of self-blame, is central to why we behave in ways we hate.

Second, causing others to suffer—that is, being the doer of bad behavior to others instead of the receiver—helps you to forget that you suffered by accommodating to your parents. Strangely enough, it is a relief being the perpetrator rather than the victim of suffering. Why? Imagine you have experienced something terrible. You want to be removed from the pain of it. The farther removed (in distance and time) you become, the safer you feel. What could be farther away than the opposite position? The position that helps to obliterate the memory of past pain is the one where you are doing the hurting instead of being hurt.

This concept, though difficult to understand, has been well documented in our prisons. In the majority of cases, child abusers, molesters, and wife beaters were abused themselves as children. Though their actions are not excusable, we can better comprehend what caused them through this concept of doing to others what was done to you.

For example, if as an adult you act possessively towards your children the way your parents were with you, it will help you to forget that you inhibited your relationships with others in order to accommodate to your possessive parents. If as an adult you dominate your children, it will help you to forget that you submitted to your domineering parents. You don't want to recall painful memories of having been cheated of your flexibility and independence.

Third, by doing to others what was done to you, you may hope that you will encounter people who can better cope with the behavior that harmed you. In this way they would become role models for you to learn new ways of dealing with behavior that was painful or difficult for you in the past.

These three reasons are why, in spite of your best intentions, you may have acquired those qualities of your parents that you hated.

All Three Responses at Work

You may find that your behavior demonstrates all three responses at different times, and therefore seems unconnected to a single problem with one or both parents. You may find that you accommodate, rebel, and do to others what was done to you at various times in your relationships.

For example, you may accommodate to and remain overly devoted to, or involved with, a possessive parent. In your relationships with others you may also feel obligated to be exceptionally devoted. However, you also may at times rebel and avoid people who want you to be close to them. And you may be possessive of your own children and jealous of their interest in other people.

In response to a domineering parent, you may be overtly respectful of authority but quietly act stubborn or defiant as your form of protest. If you act like your parent, you will be demanding and controlling toward your children and others.

CHAPTER FOUR

Why Is It Difficult to Uncover Your Mind-Sets?

LET'S LOOK AT SOME OF THE REAsons why mind-sets are so hard to uncover.

First, mind-sets are hard to uncover because they're deeply buried. Why? As children, we bury our destructive mind-sets in our unconscious mind to avoid pain much the way children bury their heads under the covers when they are afraid of ghosts.

Three Mind-Set Ghosts

THE GHOST OF PRESENT PAIN

If you try to uncover your mind-set, it may cause you pain to realize how you undermined your own success in the past. The only thing you may be aware of now is that you hate yourself for being fat or getting poor grades, and you don't know why.

Many people feel anxiety, sadness, and shame when they approach the truth about the past. These feelings make it too difficult and unpleasant to attempt the process of uncovering those mind-sets that keep us locked into unwanted behavior. Emotional discomfort is a signal beyond your awareness that you are about to behave in a way that you feel has hurt your parents in the past and may hurt them or others in the future.

THE GHOST OF PAST PAIN

Another reason we don't permit ourselves to become aware of the contents of our mind-sets is that we may become aware that we blamed ourselves for the flaws and defects of our parents or siblings that caused us to alter our development. Because it is painful to experience guilt feelings, we automatically try to block the memories that are connected with those feelings, and we do so unconsciously. After all, who wants to feel like a criminal who was responsible for wounding his or her parents and siblings. We can feel less guilty if we deny their flaws and give them credit they don't deserve.

THE GHOST OF FUTURE PAIN

If you can't recognize your mind-sets, you can't change them or the behavior that they cause. If you feel responsible for hurting someone else in the process of doing right by yourself, you will feel guilt. This guilt may cause you to feel like a criminal who should pay for his or her crimes. Therefore, you may feel you do not deserve to pursue what is good for you. This interferes with your desire to accomplish your goals. Until you overcome the power of your mind-sets by learning to understand their content and origins, you cannot change your future self-destructive behavior.

All three of these ghosts can haunt you at the same time.

The Man Haunted by His Brother's Failures

By way of example, let's take the case of a professional man named Fred who felt during childhood that his successes had ruined life for his brother (past pain). Fred's father was excessively critical of the brother, Paul, who was unsuccessful in school. Fred believed that Paul's suffering from paternal criticism was intensified by his being compared with Fred's successes. As an adult, Fred had blocked out these memories because they made him feel guilty about his sibling (present pain). Therefore, he was unable to change his pattern of undermining his successes (future pain). Pain kept Fred from recognizing his mind-set.

Remember, Fred was not responsible for his brother's difficulties. Why, then, would he blame himself for his sibling's problems when he was not at fault? By doing so he hoped to relieve his brother's suffering and his father's distress by changing or inhibiting behavior that was important to him (being an outstanding student).

How would you respond to this same situation?

DON'T GET GOOD GRADES

If, like Fred, you had the mind-set that being smart in school was threatening to the self-image of your brother, making good grades would arouse a strong sense of guilt in you. You would feel you were showing your brother up and, in that way, hurting him. As a result, you might hold yourself back from getting good grades. This behavior would be reinforced if your brother acted diminished by your success or was overtly envious of you.

Or, if you felt pressured that your father wanted you to restrain your success so your weaker brother would feel better about himself, your thinking could be, "I'd better not shine, so my father won't feel so bad about my brother." You could also hold yourself back to protect your father from feelings of shame over his failing son. In this case, your mind-set would be "Success is bad," or "Modesty is good." This code, acting like a computer virus, would restrict your behavior.

But what a price you would pay! In response to this mind-set, you would hate yourself for doing badly in school and feel like a sinner if you should somehow do well. You would experience this dilemma even though you were not, in fact, responsible for your brother's difficulties.

RESCUE YOUR BROTHER

Another way you could solve your problem would be to atone for your sin of success in school by trying to rescue your brother and any brother figures you come across in your life.

For example, you might take time out of your life to tutor your brother, even if it meant depriving yourself of enough study time. As an adult, you might become known as Mr. Rescue. If, in the process of rescuing others less fortunate you sacrificed too much of your time or otherwise harmed yourself, you would feel resentful and hate yourself for feeling this way. You would have difficulty not meeting the unreasonable requests of others. Salespeople, people needing money, or others needing help would be impossible to refuse.

The movie *Mr. Saturday Night* is a dramatic portrayal of this situation. An extremely talented and funny brother is able to make all his family members laugh. The other brother, who is shy and socially clumsy, is dragged along by the funny one to act as a straight man.

The funny brother becomes a comedian and climbs out of mediocrity to begin establishing a successful career. But he feels guilty towards his unsuccessful brother. The brother remains deferential towards him, causing the comedian to feel even more guilty.

As a result of his guilt, the comedian undermines every opportunity he has to make it big in the entertainment and television world by acting antagonistically towards those who control his destiny. This causes his career to revert back to its previous mediocre level. This obvious self-destructive behavior was motivated by the comedian's guilt towards his brother. We can assume that he had a mind-set that his success was responsible for causing his brother's lack of self-confidence.

Would Feeling Better Off Affect Me?

The sense of feeling better off than others can strongly affect us. For instance, imagine yourself in the following situation.

You are a tourist who, after visiting the sights in a poor country, sits down to eat a sumptuous meal at an outdoor restaurant in the town square. As you are eating, a group of poor, malnourished children and adults approaches to beg for money and linger nearby. Flies cover their parched lips and flit around the children's swollen bellies.

What are you feeling? How does the food taste now? As you look into one pathetic face after another, you notice a number of responses in yourself that reflect your sense of guilt about being better off.

Have you lost your appetite? Do you feel comp
the people money? Will you leave as soon as possibl
spare yourself from feeling terrible? Although in this
situation you find yourself in is short-lived, it will most likely
remain in your memory for a long time. When you recall the
event at a later date, you will reexperience the awful feelings
associated with it. That's why you'll prefer to forget it.

In the same way, we try to forget painful experiences of our
childhood. And so they remain hidden.

Why Does Behavior You Hate
Continue into Adulthood?

We often develop mind-sets as children in relation to our family
members. Why, then, do we repeat patterns that lead to bad
results, or patterns we hate, once we are adults living away from
our parents and siblings, or even after our parents are dead? Why
does the past behavior of our family members affect us when
we are no longer exposed to their negative reinforcement? Why
are our guilt feelings so difficult to overcome?

To answer these questions let's take another look at Fred.
My first meeting with Fred did not reveal the depth of his
problem, but as we talked I began to see what had caused his
difficulties.

"You seem intelligent and well-educated, Fred. Yet you say
you're a failure. How are you failing?" I asked.

"I've set up my office several times, and each time it's gone
bust," he told me.

"How do you account for that?"

"I can't. That's what's so frustrating," he admitted. "I feel
plagued by an inability to be successful. I've had great training.
I know my stuff. But when it comes to putting everything together somehow I always blow it."

"Have you always had trouble succeeding? For instance, did
you have difficulty in school, as a boy?" I asked him.

"No," he answered. "Just the opposite. My brother had
problems in that area, but I always did really well in school. In
fact, I was sort of the 'star' of our family that way. You know,
good athlete, strong learner, popular."

"Tell me about your brother," I probed.

"He's younger than me," he said. Then half sighing, with a shake of his head, he continued, "Paul always got into trouble. He misbehaved in school, even when he was really young. As a result, he always brought home terrible report cards."

"What happened at home as a result of his failures at school?" I asked.

"Dad would become enraged and eventually would beat Paul," Fred told me.

"How did you feel about that?" I wondered.

"I hated it," he confessed. "I always felt sorry for Paul. Dad would be hitting him and yelling, 'Why can't you be like your brother? Why do you always screw up?' I wished Paul could do better, too. But, more, I wished Dad would leave me out of it. It made me sick to my stomach to hear Dad yelling that way."

"How has Paul done now that he's grown?" I wondered aloud.

He frowned. "Not well. He's basically been a laborer, which would be okay. But he can't seem to do well at it. He argues with a boss and gets fired. He blows it on the job and has to leave. Naturally, that means he never has enough money to support himself. I guess I would describe Paul as the 'black sheep' of our family."

This tragic example shows how one child can be damaged by feeling guilt over the plight of his sibling and the distress of his parent. Fred developed the mind-set that his successes highlighted his brother's failure and caused Paul to be mistreated by his father.

Fred's self-destructive thinking was, "I have hurt my brother by outdoing him; therefore, I don't deserve to do well myself. I'd better keep myself down." From this experience he developed generalized feelings toward all people and situations that involved being successful and achieving for himself. Fred altered his behavior in order to overcome an unpleasant situation that was beyond his control.

Others respond to this type of sibling guilt differently from the way Fred did. They continue to do well in life but make special efforts to help or rescue those less fortunate. They experience great satisfaction from their efforts, but indirectly may resent the expense to themselves. Some people will respond in an opposite way: They become indifferent to suffering or deny that it is occurring, in order to protect themselves from feeling guilt.

If you are like Fred, you may worry that others will be hurt by your success. As a result of feeling that you hurt your sibling or parent, you might experience guilt each time you begin to do well as an adult. The guilt feeling warns you that you are violating your mind-set.

In Fred's case, the original thought, "My success hurts my brother," grew into the general idea that "It is wrong to outdo anyone." That evolved into the mind-set "Ambition is bad." As a protection, a way of hiding from the ghosts of pain, it can then become transformed into a more socially acceptable value such as "Always help others."

Although "Always help others" may be morally admirable, it can be self-destructive if you routinely sacrifice your own interests for others. But this value may be used to help conceal your real mind-set that "Ambition is bad" or "Success is wrong," thus protecting you from remembering the pain in your past that caused you to develop your hidden mind-set.

You don't know that you are burdened with a mind-set about not being successful. The only thing you are consciously aware of is your frustration at your inability to succeed. Remember, to be consciously aware of the moral value that "Success is wrong" might remind you of having hurt your sibling, feeling like a criminal, and giving up your success. Because this is painful you repress it, keeping it out of your consciousness.

The expressed value ("Always help others") is similar to the upper reaches of an iceberg. But in Fred's case, the destructive mind-set is hidden. If I assume that I have the facts when Fred says "Always help others," I will miss all that lies beneath that statement. Like an iceberg that has great capacity to damage ships by what is hidden, "Success is wrong" lies beneath the surface of Fred's consciousness. The sad irony for Fred is that because he links his own success with damaging his brother, he sinks himself in life.

Fred created failure for himself in spite of a conscious desire to succeed. Unconsciously, he thought that by failing himself, his brother's failures would no longer be highlighted.

An additional problem was that Paul's difficulties continued into adulthood, making it difficult for Fred to alter his mind-set. Paul's lack of achievement became the limiting factor for both brothers. In spite of his parents' support for his accomplishments, Fred sabotaged himself. Had Paul become successful in adult life, Fred would have felt relieved and less burdened by his feelings of guilt towards Paul.

As it was, the power of Fred's mind-set resulted in the following series of failures, in spite of his best efforts. When choosing a site for his first office, although he was advised not to, he located in an area where there were too many other practitioners for the population. After relocating to a second office, he hired too large a staff, and his practice sank under his unusually high overhead. After that failure, he tried again. This time he employed people with too little experience and found himself unable to fire those who were either incompetent or difficult to get along with.

Taken at face value, these might not seem to be obvious examples of an inability to succeed but a result of inexperience. However, Fred came to me because he knew he was unable to succeed.

There was no apparent negative reinforcement to account for Fred's behavior. Ironically, it was the positive reinforcement from his father to be successful that contributed to his self-destructiveness. If he pleased his father, he felt he would make things worse for Paul. On the other hand, by trying to save his brother pain and humiliation, he disappointed his father: a no-win situation.

Would positive advice from a standard self-help book have been helpful to Fred? Would testimonials or exercises in positive reinforcement have enabled him to overcome his destructive mind-set? His own determination and willpower weren't sufficient until Fred uncovered the hidden truths of his family history.

Before we get to the question of why will power is not enough to change the behaviors and thoughts that plague people (Chapter Nine), I am going to describe in more detail the origins of behaviors, morals, and thoughts that we hate.

CHAPTER FIVE

Mismatches Revisited

Mismatches in Childhood versus Mismatches as an Adult

In some cases, a parent's personality flaws will adversely affect a child no matter what the child's nature is. The mind-sets and conflicts that follow from a mismatch between parent and child are the results of a child's innate qualities clashing with the personalities and expectations of his or her parents and/or siblings. This is a product of fate, like a bad blind date. One example would be a daughter whose parents wanted a son.

As adults, we have many options in dealing with unpleasant people. We can get away from them or avoid them, disagree with them, or stand up for ourselves. We can divorce a miserable spouse, move away from home, take out a restraining order, get a new girlfriend or boyfriend, or see a therapist. Or we can drown our sorrows in alcohol and drugs; divert ourselves with movies, sex, or sports; or read this book and figure out what is wrong.

But what can children do to counteract their parents, who have such a powerful and paramount position in their lives? When children's innate qualities clash with those of their parents, they are too young to develop healthy coping strategies.

Instead, they respond with accommodation, rebellion, and mimicking, which are linked to future unwanted behaviors.

Let's take a look at some examples where the clash between a child's personality and his or her parents' deficiencies and peculiarities have caused problems. Do any of these mismatches apply to you? Spend some time looking at the following chart, Mismatches in Childhood (pages 44–45). It may help you to see yourself better and to learn how some of your problems may have originated. Some of the examples attribute problem behavior to a mother and some to a father. However, the gender of the parents can be interchanged in any of the examples. Later on, we will discuss each category in depth so you can better see why you may be behaving in ways you hate.

The first column describes the qualities you may have been born with and how they may clash with the personalities or character traits of one of your parents.

The second column describes what you may do in order to get along with that parent (accommodation).

The third column describes how you may defy and protest the character traits in your parent that you dislike.

The fourth column describes how, as a result of guilt, you may mimic your parent when you become an adult.

YOU ARE AN OUTGOING CHILD
WITH A WITHDRAWN MOTHER

Imagine yourself as a young child with an outgoing disposition, with a mother who is so distressed by your stimulating and lively personality that she complains to your father and the relatives about how noisy you are. What effect do you think this will have on your behavior and character? Will you continue to remain outgoing and lively, or will you subdue your feelings and enthusiasm? You might develop the mind-set "Being lively causes Mother to become burdened, irritated, and rejecting."

Bill's mother was a restrained, quiet, cautious woman who isolated herself from people and immersed herself in gardening and reading. She was unprepared for the disruption in her emotional life when Bill was born. Later on, he was told by his father that he was a raucous, outgoing, lively, and noisy child from day one, who jarred her serenity and composure. She complained that Bill was a handful for her. She didn't react to her frustration with anger, but instead withdrew and occasionally cried about her inability to cope with her son.

What would you do if you were like Bill when you were a child?

If You Accommodate   What do you imagine would be the outcome? To protect his mother from becoming hurt by him, Bill developed a destructive mind-set that forced him to restrain his enthusiasm, hide his feelings, and make himself subdued. By doing so he blocked or restricted important aspects of his personality, which remained blocked as an adult. When he grew up, Bill hated himself for being so cautious, introverted, and restricted from being able to have fun and be spontaneous. He hated himself even more for not being able to change his behavior. These were Bill's major complaints when he went into therapy.

If You Rebel   If you took the rebellious path, you would deliberately act overenthusiastic, boisterous, loud, and outlandish, both as your way of rebelling as well as a way to try to make your mother realize that her attitude was bad for you and that it ought to stop. Retaining this kind of behavior as an adult might make you be seen as provocative and rude and could dampen your chances of forming lasting relationships or being promoted at work. Fortunately for Bill, he expressed his rebelliousness by humorously mimicking others, without being overly provocative.

If You Do to Others What Was Done to You   As an adult, if you do to your kids what was done to you, you may find yourself being criticized by your kids for being an introvert or a grouch who doesn't have fun. Taking on your mother's traits without being aware of it is payment for causing her to be burdened by you as a child. By discouraging your children from acting lively, you would be doing to them what was done to you; therefore, you wouldn't have to remember and re experience what was painful to you.

In addition, you may treat your peers the way your mother treated you to see if they are better able to handle it than you were. If they are, you will have found role models for yourself.

MISMATCHES IN CHILDHOOD

What You Are	You Accommodate and Inhibit Yourself	You Rebel and Protest	You Do to Others / What Was Done to You
You are outgoing or overly expansive, but your laid-back parent is provoked.	You become subdued and introverted.	You become wild, outlandish, and uncontrolled.	You inhibit your children or others from being expressive and outgoing.
You are quiet, whereas your parent needs stimulation.	You feel you have to perform, entertain, or be outspoken.	You remain shy, withdrawn, and quiet.	You insist that your children or others perform for you. You become angry if they are quiet.
You are not affectionate or responsive enough to your parent's need to love you.	You feel you have to be overly affectionate and accept everything your parent offers.	You reject affection, closeness, and guidance from others	You are overly loving and baby your children.
You are the wrong sex. Your parent is very disappointed.	You inhibit your sexuality and act more like the opposite sex. You have low self-esteem.	You act hypermasculine if you are rejected for being a boy, and vice versa. Nothing is your fault.	You are disappointed with your child's sex. You are antagonistic to those of a particular sex.

You are laid back, but your parent demands achievement.	You feel driven to succeed and are anxious about exams and competing. You fear failing.	You deliberately do poorly at whatever your parent expects you to achieve.	You demand achievement from your children and are perfectionistic with others.
You are born disabled, and your parent is burdened, resentful, or ashamed.	You try to hide your deficiency at all costs, and you feel guilty about receiving help for your problem.	You flaunt your disability and try to shame your parents.	You are insensitive to suffering in others. You make fun of people's deficiencies.
You're adventurous, but your parent is overprotective and fearful of danger.	You become cautious and inhibited about sports, activities, and new situations.	You throw caution to the wind, become a risk taker, and use poor judgment about dangerous situations.	You are overprotective with your children and worry about danger everywhere.
You are delightful, but your parent is indifferent or jealous.	You act subdued, avoid the limelight, and defer to others.	You refuse to give credit to others. You go out of your way to get recognition.	You are indifferent to the achievements of others.

YOU ARE A QUIET CHILD WITH A
MOTHER WHO NEEDS STIMULATION

What happens if you are born naturally quiet or shy but your mother is depressed and needy of stimulation? Consider what strategy you would have to develop to accommodate to her and the effect that it would have on you. Your unconscious mind-set could be "Playing by myself or having fun with my friends causes Mother to be depressed."

What could you do?

If You Accommodate   You might force yourself to be more outgoing and entertaining as a child even though it causes you pain. When you grow up, you might feel obligated to take care of others or make them happy at your own expense. Or you might find yourself forced to always be cheerful and happy, never revealing your true feelings. Will you hate yourself for being over solicitous of your spouse and others?

If You Rebel   As a child, you might refuse to talk and might withdraw from your mother. This would probably cause great guilt, because you would see her increased distress and you would feel responsible for it. To defend yourself against the burden of feeling obligated to worry about others as an adult, you could easily isolate yourself from intimate relationships and develop interests that are not people-oriented. You might find yourself bristling whenever anyone, including your spouse, children, and friends, wanted attention from you.

If You Do to Others What Was Done to You   As an adult, you might find yourself dissatisfied with your children, your mate, and your friends and coworkers if they are shy or quiet.

Sherman, a business consultant who came to me because he was depressed, wasn't aware that his low moods were instigated by his own destructive mind-set. He was always accommodating to others, not because he was trying to be a good guy, but because he felt obligated to make others feel good. What a burden that obligation caused! He resented this in himself, but felt inhibited from activities that made him happy. He felt guilty about enjoying his life.

Sherman's attitudes were carried over from childhood experiences with his mother, who depended on him for stimulation. He was a quiet, reserved child who felt forced to act more lively to make his mother feel better. She was a depressed woman who was ignored by her husband and looked to her son for stimulation. Sherman was caught between resentment about making others happy at his expense and guilty feelings about making himself happy because he believed his enjoyment caused others to suffer.

YOU ARE NOT AFFECTIONATE OR RESPONSIVE ENOUGH TO YOUR PARENT'S NEED TO LOVE YOU

Think of what it would be like if you were a child whose mother blamed herself because you were colicky, sick, or allergic to milk. If you resisted her attempts to feed you, her reaction might be to feel inadequate and/or rejected by you. As a result, she might try hard to be affectionate to compensate for her hurt feelings.

"Come on, take the bottle, honey. Mama wants you to eat. I love you so much. Don't you want to eat for Mama?" Even though you wouldn't be able to tell her so, you might feel she was suffocating you with her affection.

What could you do?

If You Accommodate   You might develop a mind-set that would require you to do more to please your mother, such as "Rejecting my mother hurts her, so I will always accept everything she offers."

Imagine the behavior that would develop in response to this destructive mind-set! You would have to eat everything set in front of you. You would have to allow her to baby you. You might have to hide feeling upset in order to maintain her sense of fulfillment as a mother. You would have difficulty saying no to anyone. As an adult, you might be disgusted with yourself for being a "soft touch" for every salesman who comes knocking on your door. You would hate yourself for having to go to great lengths to make other people feel worthwhile.

Jonathan was caught in such a bind. For the first few years of his life he experienced repeated stomach cramps as a result of an unknown allergy to milk and orange juice. The more he cried, the more milk his mother fed him in order to comfort him. As a result, he caused her to feel inadequate and guilty. She compensated by being as affectionate as possible, always looking for acknowledgment that she was in fact a good parent. Although this was not the only source of his later difficulties, it contributed to Jonathan's problems with accommodation and rebellion. He felt obligated to "go along" in order to make others feel worthwhile, but at the same time he maintained his emotional distance. He was afraid of becoming too subservient to others, particularly the women he dated.

If You Rebel   What do you think would happen if you resisted your mother's heavy-handed attempt to give you affection? If you resented having to accept what others offered, you could rebel against this mind-set by rejecting affection, closeness, or guidance from others. Think about how this behavior would undermine your life. You'd always be pushing people away, and you'd wonder why you could never develop any lasting, intimate relationships.

If You Do to Others What Was Done to You   If you identified with your mother's behavior toward you, you would most likely baby others and make it difficult for your children to become independent of you.

Some parents discourage their children from leaving home because their sense of meaning and purpose is derived from nurturing their offspring. If your parents acted that way, you would feel guilty for not needing them at a time when they still wanted to baby you. You would feel that you were hurting them by depriving them of their sense of meaning in life.

I treated Penny, a freshman college student, for depression and poor scholastic performance. Her friends kept telling her that she was homesick and that she would get over it. But she didn't, because it was her parents who were actually homesick for her, their only child. She felt guilty about not needing them as she did when she was younger. When she became aware of this hidden dynamic, her depression disappeared.

YOU ARE A GIRL, BUT YOUR PARENTS WANTED A BOY

Is there a wrong sex? Of course not. But if one or both of your parents wanted a child of the opposite sex, fate has dealt you both a bad card. Your parent might have been a great one for a boy, and you might have been the perfect match for a parent wanting a girl. As it is, you are mismatched. What kind of mind-set do you suppose you would develop if you were not the sex your parents preferred?

If You Accommodate If you were a girl, but your parents expected and preferred a boy, you might develop the mind-set "Being feminine disappoints my parents, so I'd better be tough and masculine." When you grew up and found yourself automatically controlled by this mind-set, would you hate yourself for inhibiting your feminine side? If you are still able to accomplish feminine pursuits, will you feel uneasy and unfulfilled in the process? Perhaps you'll be mad at yourself for not letting yourself feel happy in your relationships with men. Some people might go so far as to have a sex-change operation.

If You Rebel What if you rebelled against suppressing your femininity, and instead found yourself acting compulsively promiscuous and hating yourself for it? Behaving in a promiscuous way might be a reaction of defiance to a mind-set that you should suppress your femininity.

If You Did to Others What Was Done to You If you identified with your parents' behavior towards you in order to relieve your guilt towards them, you might be disappointed with the sex of your own child. This would serve as self-punishment for having disappointed them. In addition, this identification with your parents would help you to repress your memories of having been mistreated by them. Mistreating others helps you to repress the memories of your own mistreatment.

I treated a twenty-eight-year-old nurse named Cynthia for a generalized sense of unhappiness. The more she divulged her childhood history, the more clearly I saw that she was battling her natural feminine inclinations.

ynthia first came to see me she complained about
ships with men.

t relax and just enjoy myself," she explained.

t do you mean?" I wondered.

"Well, in particular, I'm always really aggressive about sex—
I want to initiate, you know. But if I get into a relationship with
a guy and he begins to pursue me sexually, I don't like it."

"Do you feel threatened or frightened?" I asked her.

"No, just irritated. I resent it totally," she said. "I want to
be in charge!"

After I helped her recover memories of her parents' disap-
pointment about her not being a boy, she began to face her feelings of unworthiness and low self-esteem (that she wasn't loved
for herself).

One day she began to cry. "What's making you cry?" I asked.

"I just realized," she said. "It isn't me. I mean . . . it never
was. My parents wanted a boy and I was a girl. They rejected
me for something I had no control over. It was never my fault."

Cynthia began to understand why relationships had always
been a problem for her. If she allowed herself to be pursued
(which was what she really wanted), she felt she was rebelling
against her parents by behaving in a "feminine" manner. That
made her feel guilty, causing her to reject men who pursued her.

When she acted in a "masculine" way by initiating sex with
men, she felt resentful about having to violate her true nature.

YOU ARE RELAXED, BUT YOUR
FATHER DEMANDS ACHIEVEMENT

Imagine the frustration and anxiety you would feel if you
weren't driven to be a great achiever when your father was intense about those issues and needed you to achieve in order for
him to feel worthwhile.

What are your choices?

If You Accommodate   Your mind-set might be "I have to try
harder to be perfect, because otherwise Dad will be disappointed
and angry." You might feel obligated to push yourself beyond
your abilities or proclivities and feel anxious about failing. You

might find it difficult to relax or allow yourself to make mistakes. You may find that your father is never satisfied, no matter how great your success. His self-esteem is so tied up with your success that it is difficult for you to be yourself.

If You Rebel   You might deliberately fail, hoping that your father will get the message and stop demanding achievement from you.

If You Do to Others What Was Done to You   As payment for disappointing your father, you might become a perfectionist with your own children and always be disappointed with their performances.

Robin, one of my clients, was a very dynamic administrator who had become an extremely organized achiever in order to please her father. Although she was successful in many endeavors, she was always unhappy because she felt that she was never achieving for herself. Her successes were always for some other purpose. She felt some gratification from pleasing her father, but she never felt loved for herself. Her achievements were not really her own.

Robin had occasional periods of depression associated with times when she felt unsuccessful in realizing some standard of perfection. She hated herself for feeling so driven and perfectionistic. Conversely, she also hated herself for not feeling free to relax and do things at a comfortable pace. Once she recognized her mind-sets she became happier.

Robin might have rebelled by failing in school and work as a protest against having to perform. Doing so would have been an attempt to make her father realize that his behavior was provocative and detrimental to her.

YOU HAVE A DISABILITY AND YOUR PARENTS ARE RESENTFUL

If you are born with a physical or mental disability and your parents are ashamed and resentful about the special care and attention you need, you may develop a mind-set that will cause you to experience emotional problems as an adult.

What can you do?

If You Accommodate   Your disability may cause you guilt for burdening your parents. Your mind-set might be "I've spoiled my parents' life, and therefore I don't deserve to have things go my way." In response to this, you could easily keep yourself from fulfilling your life goals. You probably would make strong efforts to hide or compensate for your disability to relieve the burden on your parents.

If your parents' self-esteem is injured by your deficiency (they are ashamed of you because you make them look bad), you will probably experience blame and punish yourself with feelings of low self-esteem (you will feel ashamed). If you think your disability is diverting your parents' attention from your siblings and causing them to resent you, you will probably feel guilty and feel obliged to suffer for it. You might, for example, prevent yourself from having fulfilling relationships with people as penance for depriving your siblings of fulfilling relationships with your parents.

If you think being a burden is causing friction between your parents, you may, as an adult, pay by preventing yourself from having a good marriage. In addition, you may also find it very difficult to feel deserving of accepting any help because you are afraid that you will be perceived as a burden. Therefore, you may suppress your complaints and suffer quietly. Finally, in response to your sense of guilt, you may find yourself making sacrifices for your family, no matter what the cost to you.

If You Rebel   You might flaunt your disability and act outrageously, hoping your parents will realize your need for acceptance. Or you might push for your needs to be met at all costs to your family, becoming arrogant and demanding.

If You Do to Others What Was Done to You   You might show indifference to the complaints of others, or even make fun of those who are disabled.

YOU ARE ADVENTUROUS, BUT YOUR MOTHER IS OVERPROTECTIVE

If you were an adventurous child with an overly worried parent who sees danger in every situation, then reacts by being overly restrictive, what could you do?

If You Accommodate   You may think, "My mother becomes disturbed whenever I'm out of her sight, so I'd better never venture out. There is danger everywhere." You might suffer from feeling overly fearful, develop phobias, and refuse to go to school. Thinking you are hurting your parents by not restricting yourself enough could inhibit you from participating in sports or cause you to feel shy about new situations.

If You Rebel   You could become extremely wild and daring, going to the opposite extreme to send a clear message of protest: "Leave me alone and let me live!" As we have already discussed in an earlier example, you might seriously harm yourself as a result.

If You Do to Others What Was Done to You   As an adult, you might restrict your own children and torture yourself by worrying about them getting hurt, as punishment for having caused your parents so much worry. This way you would be paying yourself back for the trouble you caused your parents to experience. Remember the primitive tribe? They too have to atone for the trouble they caused their gods.

A teenaged girl named Tina was referred to me because of a severe drinking problem that was creating difficulties for her in social and school activities. The major underlying cause was her rebellion against her mother, who had been extremely overprotective of Tina since early childhood. Because she accommodated to her mother's overprotectiveness, Tina had difficulty separating from her mother, beginning with preschool. General unhappiness in school, crying, and wanting to come home were common symptoms at that time. She developed the destructive mind-set that her mother didn't want her to have fun.

As Tina got older, her mother continued to be very restrictive, causing Tina to feel angry and frustrated. She could have interpreted her mother's worry about danger to mean that she was concerned about her. But because her mother's protectiveness was extreme, Tina instead felt guilty about having fun because she saw that it hurt, provoked, and upset her mother. Therefore, Tina had to be self-destructive in order to have a good time. Her drinking was not only a form of rebellion against the restrictiveness she felt, but it allowed her to release her inhibitions and have fun without feeling responsible for her own behavior.

Once she was able to understand that she was struggling to overcome the mind-set "It is wrong to have fun and be adventuristic," Tina stopped drinking. As it became clearer to her that she wasn't responsible for her mother's unhappiness and that her mother's over-protectiveness was her own problem, Tina felt freer to have fun with her friends. She realized that she had been holding herself back to placate her mother and drinking to rebel against holding herself back. If Tina had not discovered her hidden mind-set, she might have grown up to identify with her mother's behavior. When she herself became a parent she might have been overprotective with her children as punishment for the worry she caused her own mother to suffer.

YOU ARE DELIGHTFUL, BUT YOUR FATHER IS INDIFFERENT OR ENVIOUS

Imagine the mind-set that would result if you had a delightful, charming personality, but your father was indifferent to you.

What could you do?

If You Accommodate   You might react with a belief that "When people pay attention to me, father is hurt. Therefore, it is best to act subdued, stay out of the limelight, and not draw attention to myself." In response to this mind-set you could see yourself as always second best, deferring to others so they could shine in your place.

If You Rebel   Instead, you might take center stage and be boastful, flaunting your abilities in an attempt to give your father the message that he is damaging your development.

If You Do to Others What Was Done to You   You might act just like your father so that he won't notice any difference between the two of you. If a parent is competitive or envious, there is an additional motive to copy him or her. If you are just like your parent, he or she has nothing to be envious of. To avoid remembering the pain of how you stifled yourself as a child, as an adult you might mimic your father and be indifferent to or envious of your own children. You would then hate yourself for not being a caring father or mother.

A young lawyer named Dan came to me after he had been fired from his job. He was a very talented man who unconsciously held himself back from fulfilling his potential. He had always been a bright student and was much admired by his mother and other relatives.

However, Dan's father was indifferent to him and didn't acknowledge either his intellectual ability or charm. Why? Because he was envious of his son. The father's poor self-image seemed connected to his status as a financially unsuccessful tradesman who had only a high school education. Dan developed the destructive mind-set "Father feels threatened by me, so I have to make him feel better by not calling attention to myself."

Dan responded to this by keeping others from noticing his intellectual and personal abilities. As a result, he remained ineffective in many ways, which caused him to eventually be fired from his job.

Therapy helped Dan to recognize how his father's lifelong attitude had caused him to inhibit himself and how his guilt about standing out made him act in self-defeating ways. Recognizing his destructive mind-set helped Dan to overcome suppressing his abilities.

What Are the Consequences of Mismatches?

In summary, there are three ways you may have responded as a child if you were mismatched with one or both parents.

1. You might have accommodated to your parents' faults in order to feel loved by them, thereby relieving your guilt at having hurt them by not fulfilling their expectations.
2. You might have rebelled against accommodating to your parents in order to fight their unconscious or overt attempts to curtail your development.
3. You might have grown up to be like your parents and behave the same way toward your own spouse, children, and others. *The principle is that if you caused your*

parents or siblings to suffer (and like the primitive tribe, you believe you have), then you deserve to suffer the same way. This dynamic of self-blame is central to why you become like them and behave in ways you hate.

Additionally, you may find that your behavior will demonstrate all three responses at different times, further confusing the issue.

Now let's look more specifically at how destructive mindsets are developed in childhood.

CHAPTER SIX

Who . . .
Me?

Why Children Tend to Assume
Blame for Their Parents' Mistakes

As an adult, when you meet someone who is weird, offensive, or antagonistic, you probably don't blame yourself for that person's behavior. Instead, you think to yourself, "That person is strange!" You also might be inclined to confirm with someone else that your impressions of the odd person are correct.

This is not how children respond to such behavior, however. *Children often blame themselves for their parents' bad behavior and form mind-sets that are destructive.* However, in order to diminish their sense of guilt, children will also give their parents more credit than they deserve, deny their flaws, or focus on their good qualities.

Even parents who consistently act badly in some specific fashion can function properly in other areas of life. For example, a parent who is overprotective can still promote other aspects of your development such as encouraging you to get good grades or to get along well with your siblings and/or other parent. If the same parent pays attention to your other needs, it will help to make you feel worthwhile. If that parent demonstrates skill in other areas, such as getting along with people, he or she will be setting a good example for you to follow. This helps to modify any impairment to your healthy development.

In an average family situation, where a parent's behavior toward a child is not extreme over the years, there is usually little conflict between the behavior of the parent and that of the child.

However, when a mother, father, or sibling has a consistently provocative, antagonistic, rejecting, or frustrating attitude toward a child, the child will unconsciously try to solve the problem by changing his or her own behavior.

What accounts for this?

First, children see the world from a very narrow perspective. This is because they lack experience in dealing with adults. Children assume that what is important to their parents is also paramount to other adults. Their world of relationships consists primarily of their parents and possibly their siblings, and therefore they assume that other people are like the members of their family.

With no previous life experience, there is no way of judging how things ought to be. It's difficult for a child to know whether his or her parents are behaving badly because of the parents' nature or because of something the child has done. As a result, a child is unable to make the appropriate connections between cause and effect.

You Make It Up to Them by Spoiling Your Life

Earlier we used the analogy of a primitive tribe trying to appease the gods in the hope of controlling natural disasters. When you were a child, any turmoil in your home was a natural disaster. Since your parents were crucial to your life, you had very powerful motives to understand the problems you were faced with and to solve them. Therefore, you carefully scrutinized your behavior, hoping to discover the reason your parents were upset. After all, the only variable that you had control over was your own behavior. That was what you probably tried to adjust in hopes of relieving your problem.

If you assumed that you caused the disturbance (or natural disaster) that spoiled the sense of comfort you had in your family, you probably tried to change your behavior in an attempt to overcome or control what was disturbing to you.

Again, to return to an earlier example, children are like an employee hired by a company and given no information about the job. The employee hasn't a clue about what the job entails or how to do it well. But she or he desperately needs this job! *Why is the boss scowling? I don't know! Did I do something wrong? Is he angry with me? What am I supposed to do anyway?*

Too little information would cause the employee to seize every shred of information he or she could find. So let's imagine that you are a child and your father, like the boss in the previous example, is always angry with you. You don't know why. Therefore, you watch and assess:

Mother comes over and hugs me. She makes a fuss over how cute I am. Father scowls in our direction. Maybe Father doesn't like it when Mother loves me. Maybe he wants her to hug him instead. That's why he yells at me! He's jealous. That must be what's wrong with him!

If you believe that your father is continually mad at you because your mother adores you, you could easily distance yourself from her and develop a general belief that involvements with women are dangerous.

Or, in a different case, if your mind-set is that your father is angry with you because you aren't achieving in school or sports, it can cause you to feel great anxiety whenever you have to perform or undertake a new activity. You might develop a mind-set to avoid competition of any kind, for fear of failing and making your father angry with you.

If instead you conclude that your father is angry because he resents your endearing personality, you could easily inhibit your charm and become unappealing.

If you decide your father's anger is caused by the fact that you aren't interested enough in him, you may feel obligated to spend time with him or to always put his interests first.

If you feel he is angry because he needs to put you down in order to feel superior, you may feel obligated to act inferior.

Whatever was amiss, as a child you probably took the blame and tried to come up with a way to make things right. Remember, this was an unconscious process. But the belief that you had somehow hurt your parent had the power to prevent you from expressing your true nature and achieving your dreams and wishes.

As an adult, you have enough experience with people to ascertain whether you are or are not to blame for a conflict with someone. You know when you are being lax or performing well. Before accepting a job, you would ordinarily acquire information about the company, the boss, and what is expected of you to do your job properly. You would know whether the criticism you received from your boss was justified or not.

If the criticism was justified, instead of it causing you to change your behavior in a way that was self-destructive, you would simply do the job better. If that somehow wasn't sufficient, you could always leave and get another job. The reason you could make the decision to improve or to leave is because you are able to make the proper assumptions about cause and effect: whether it is you or your boss who is responsible for the problem.

As a child, the mind-sets that you develop from early experiences become encoded in your unconscious mind. You then live the rest of your life according to them! All your life these mind-sets will cause you to repeat problem behavior with people, even if they are in conflict with or spoil what works for you in the world outside your family. Furthermore, once they are established, you can't reevaluate their validity because of their hidden nature. Rather, you continue living according to them whether they are true or not.

Imagine a doctor who performed surgery based only on the information available twenty years ago! Or a lawyer defending a client based on law practices that are outdated! We constantly incorporate new information in our work. But in our personal lives, where guilt holds our unconscious mind-sets in place, our thinking remains like that of a child or a primitive tribe.

Operating according to childhood mind-sets on an ongoing basis occurs because we continue to assume that our actions will hurt and provoke others, just as we think they did our parents and siblings. Therefore, we block our own goals and successes and inhibit the development of our personal and social skills.

As children, any behavior that makes us feel we have hurt our parents or siblings makes us feel guilt, shame, or anxiety. As adults, any behavior that reminds us of those past experiences and their attendant unpleasant emotions is processed through our mind-sets and dealt with as they were during childhood. These emotions short-circuit attempts at changing our actions or recognizing our beliefs and changing them.

Like a dog with an electronic collar who experiences an electric shock whenever he approaches a particular boundary, the intensity of the emotions increases the closer you get to the kind of behavior you thought hurt your parents or siblings.

God Gave Moses Ten Commandments; You Create Your Own

Were you raised with the Ten Commandments? If so, they probably still influence your actions. Because you were taught that certain behavior is unlawful, you tend to inhibit it. Violation of the law makes you aware of the guilt of having committed a sin. The Ten Commandments consist of a limited number of moral commands. The other moral commands are composed of demands on your behavior by your mind-sets.

Mind-sets function in a similar way to limit your behavior. When you violate their laws, you feel as if you are committing a sin. How does this work?

When responding to the biblical commandment "Thou shalt not steal," you don't have to go through the process of thinking out loud, "It is wrong to steal." This value is encoded in your unconscious mind and makes you automatically feel that it is wrong to steal. Any temptation to transgress causes you to experience a sense of guilt, which, like the signal from an electronic dog collar, keeps your behavior within the boundaries defined by your mind-set. In other words, it keeps you honest.

Eventually, the commandment "Thou shalt not steal" becomes transformed into a positive value, "It is good to be honest." Now you feel proud of your sense of honesty and you avoid unpleasant guilt feelings. "It is good to be honest" is one step removed from the thought "Thou shalt not steal." This is another reason why mind-sets become hidden. The positive thought "It is good to be honest" is like the ice at the top of the iceberg. Submerged beneath, unseen, lies the law "Thou shalt not steal."

This is exactly how you respond in relation to the commandments of your own mind-sets when you are tempted to transgress them. The ten biblical commandments relate to the family of humankind. Most people agree with them. Your own personal commandments developed within the confines of your family but operate in your mind with the same authority as the Ten Commandments.

Obeying Your Personal Commandments

If you have the mind-set "Disloyalty is wrong because it hurts my mother," you could avoid becoming too involved with your father, siblings, or other people significant to you. Eventually, this mind-set, peculiar to your family, could lead to the more positive thought, "Loyalty is good." "Loyalty is good" is one step removed from the negative mind-set "Disloyalty is wrong because it hurts my mother."

By living your life according to this more positive rule, you will feel less stressed emotionally. Doing so spares you from experiencing unpleasant guilt signals and painful memories that would be triggered by your hidden, negative mind-set. It also keeps you from remembering self-destructive ways in which you had to behave in order to accommodate to your mother.

Because you have hidden the source of your past pain and the cause of your present behavior, it is hard to change your behavior, no matter how good the self-help advice is, and no matter how hard you try.

The transformation of a negative mind-set into a positive one means that you don't have to feel guilty for having been disloyal to your mother. You have a positive moral commandment that guides your behavior. This command brings its own justification. By being proud of behaving according to your moral commandment you have spared yourself memories of having to be overly loyal, of compromising your independence, and of experiencing guilt for wanting to be independent and pain because of being forced to behave according to expectations. You may feel proud of yourself, keep behaving in ways you hate.

If you have a hidden disloyalty mind-set, you may find it difficult to leave home or to be successful in establishing lasting ties with others. Lasting relationships may be impaired because you fear, as with your parent, that you will be required to be loyal to your new partner to the point of becoming trapped. You may find it difficult to have a successful relationship with another person because this causes you to feel disloyal to your parent.

Amazingly, you may even find fault with one parent in order to maintain your loyalty to the other.

The struggle over whether to put an aged parent in a nursing home is never an easy decision. However, if you have a hidden disloyalty mind-set, you will probably have great difficulty putting your parent in a nursing home, even if it is truly the right thing to do. Attempting to make that decision will arouse strong guilt feelings. All you will be aware of, however, is how painful the experience is.

If your parent was rejecting when you wanted to be close, you could create a new commandment: "Don't ask for too much attention," which becomes transformed into "Independence is good." If you have this kind of hidden mind-set, you may find it difficult to experience closeness because you fear rejection.

Summary

Mind-sets are created in relation to your parents and siblings to help you maintain your ties to your family. These negative rules can become part of your unconscious mind so that you automatically behave in ways that you think will not hurt or disturb your parents or siblings. In the process, you may develop new moral commandments that operate all your life. Throughout your adult life you may continue to behave in ways that you think will not hurt others, similar to the ways you avoided hurting your parents or siblings.

As a child, your limited perspective caused you to blame yourself for your family's faults. Because your view of cause and effect was similar to that of a primitive tribe, you concluded that you must change your behavior to overcome the problem. As you

HOW YOU CREATE NEW MORAL COMMANDMENTS

The Behavior of Your Parents or Siblings	They Are Hurt and Disturbed	Your Mind-Set Thoughts to Please Them Are	Your New Moral Commands Are
They are authoritative and need to be in control.	When you act independently and defy their authority.	"It is best to follow their rules and to do what I am told."	Obedience is good.
They are rejecting when you want to be close or affectionate.	When you want to be close or have other needs to be taken care of.	"It is wrong to be dependent, close, or intimate with them."	Independence is good.
They are possessive and need you to be involved with them over others.	When you are involved with or think highly of other people.	"It is wrong to be separate, keep my distance from them, or value others highly."	Loyalty is good.
They are self-centered and competitive with you.	When you try to be noticed, admired, or successful.	"It is wrong to stand out or to be accomplished."	Modesty and restraint are good.
They are depressed and needy.	When you don't sacrifice for them, take care of them, or feel sorry for them.	"It is wrong to focus on making myself happy."	Saving and rescuing the downtrodden are good.
They are failing in school or work.	When you are doing well.	"It is wrong to succeed and outdo them."	Being nice to others is good.
They live through your accomplishments.	When you fail to succeed or stand out.	"It is wrong to fail or make mistakes. It is wrong to not drive myself."	Success is everything.

They are unpredictable. They use drugs or alcohol.	When you speak up to confront them or demand reliability.	"Don't make demands or expect parenting."	Self-reliance and control are best.
They are overly critical.	When you refuse to accept blame.	"I'm at fault whatever the criticism."	Be perfect. Never make mistakes.
They are overprotective.	When you are wild, take chances, or are reckless.	"It is wrong to be adventurous."	Caution is best.
They are underprotective.	When you are watchful, wary, and cautious.	"It is wrong to be cautious."	Risk is good.
They are amoral.	When you do what is right and honest.	"It is wrong to be moral."	Dishonesty is best. Get what you want, no matter what. The ends justify the means.
They are very self-righteous, moralistic, and disdainful.	When you don't follow the straight and narrow.	"It is wrong to disobey the rules or cause them shame."	Righteousness above all.

continued in life, your mind-sets stayed with you and continued to influence your behavior.

The accompanying chart, How You Create New Moral Commandments (pages 64–65), will show how your parents or siblings may respond when you don't accommodate to them, the mind-sets you develop in order to make them feel better, and the resulting moral commandments that follow. These new commandments can be responsible for guiding much of your behavior throughout life.

We have just examined the mind-sets that can result from mismatches between parent and child. In the next chapter, we will discuss defects in parents that are hurtful no matter what qualities a child is born with. These examples, as well as the charts that summarize them, are ways to discover how and why you developed and maintain behaviors you hate. In Chapter Eleven, I will provide additional ways to create profiles of you and your family members and how to use this information to change what you dislike.

CHAPTER SEVEN

Your Bad Experiences Were Real, Not Imagined

We Correctly Evaluate Our Parents and Siblings

All families have problems. Destructive mind-sets, however, are caused by extreme family problems that persist for a considerable period of time. In order to fulfill our inborn biologicalpsychological destiny, we need a reasonably nurturing environment that will promote our aptitudes, talents, sensibilities, ambition, and goals. From the day we are born, we want to spread our wings and fly. It is nature's law that we become as strong as possible and be equipped as best we can to leave the nest. The specific parent or sibling defects described in this chapter will cause harm no matter what qualities a child is born with, serving to clip the child's wings.

If you see members of your family hurt by your behavior, you will inhibit yourself even at the expense of your best interests. You don't want to suffer the guilt of hurting them, disappointing them, provoking them, and worrying them. Instead, you alter your own behavior in an unconscious attempt to keep the family unit together and functioning smoothly. The outcome may not be what you'd expect because so much of the contribution to your behavior remains hidden.

We are equipped to know, even unconsciously, whether our parent or sibling is reacting to us from a position of strength or weakness. It is too important to our development not to perceive our experiences with them correctly. If a parent is hurt by our behavior, we will inhibit ourselves even at the expense of our best interests. From this it follows that we are strongly motivated to assess them correctly.

To prevent yourself from unnecessarily spoiling your life, you will not be inclined to mistake bluster, authority, and self-centeredness for strength. Similarly, you are not likely to perceive possessiveness, overprotectiveness, and living through your accomplishments as true interests and concern for you. Depression and neediness won't be misperceived for kindness and sensitivity. You are unlikely to believe that emotional coldness and rejection are signs of character and self-discipline.

Therefore, the responses of accommodation, rebellion, self-blame, and identification are the result of real, not imagined, flaws, deficiencies, and mistreatments by your parents and siblings.

The chart that comes next is called How to Discover the Cause of Your Problems (pages 69–71). Identify the quality of the parent or sibling you disliked the most, and who caused the most difficulty for you. By using the first example of a controlling, authoritarian parent, you can see how that parent affected your behavior if you responded by accommodating, rebelling, or mimicking.

If you aren't clear about how to profile either you or your parents in the chart How to Discover the Cause of Your Problems, reading Chapter Eleven at any time should help. In Chapter Eleven, Finding Your Skeletons, I present several questions to help you create personality profiles of you and your family members.

Once you have located on the chart which parental qualities apply to your situation, you will find in the material that follows detailed explanations and clinical examples that will amplify the origins of the behavior you hate.

HOW TO DISCOVER THE CAUSE OF YOUR PROBLEMS

Your Parent or Sibling Is	When You Accommodate to Their Bad Behavior	When You Rebel and Protest Against What They Expect	When You Become Like Your Parent and Do to Others What Was Done to You
Controlling and authoritarian	You overrespect authority, are conservative, unspontaneous, and obey the rules.	You are stubborn, resist demands, and refuse to give in. Your values conflict with theirs.	You are bossy, demanding, and controlling and expect strict obedience to you and the rules.
Rejecting	You are self-reliant and avoid needing people. You avoid showing feelings. Closeness to others feels risky.	You insist on having your demands met. You may act destructively to get attention.	You are indifferent to others and enjoy seeing them hurt or hurting them yourself.
Physically abusive	You feel unworthy and guilt-ridden. You will do anything to please.	You try to fight back as long as possible. You become rebellious and angry and have a chip on your shoulder.	You physically abuse others the way you were abused.
Possessive	You are overly loyal and feel afraid of being separate.	You reject demands made on you. You keep your distance from people who want to be close to you. You fear being taken advantage of.	You suffocate others. You feel jealous of attention paid to others. You may become violent in a jealous rage.

HOW TO DISCOVER THE CAUSE OF YOUR PROBLEMS, Continued

Your Parent or Sibling Is	When You Accommodate to Their Bad Behavior	When You Rebel and Protest Against What They Expect	When You Become Like Your Parent and Do to Others What Was Done to You
Competitive and self-centered	You are afraid to speak up or be the center of attention. You frustrate your successes and accomplishments.	You refuse to give credit to others' accomplishments. You go out of your way to get recognition and attention.	You put others down and enjoy their faults and failures. You need to be the center of attention.
Depressed and needy	You feel guilty about being happy. You tend to feel sorry for and rescue the needy. You have to help others before you can feel good.	You keep distant from anyone who is needy and unhappy. You become insensitive to others.	No one can please you. You suffer and complain all the time. You feel and appear grim to others.
Weak and ineffectual	You may feel that you have to be strong, take charge, act decisively.	You ignore problems in others and let them flounder.	You have no backbone. You are meek and give in to what others want.
Living through your accomplishments	You feel great pressure to do well or be perfect. You fear failure. You feel anxious when you try to relax.	You hide your accomplishments and live an understated life. You deliberately fail.	You use people and take credit for what they do. You expect perfection and are overly critical of mistakes in others.

On alcohol or drugs and is unpredictable and/or violent	You become vigilant and alert. You will inhibit yourself to avoid setting them off. You will feel unprotected and insecure and have to be the parent.	You act hateful towards anyone not in control. You may become insensitive to suffering in others.	You are unpredictable, explosive, and unreliable. You will probably become a drug user.
Critical	You have low self-esteem, accept blame easily, have self-critical thoughts (I'm lazy, selfish, no good, etc.). You may feel there is no use trying.	You are feisty and rebellious and deny anything is ever your fault.	You are quick to blame others even when they have done no wrong.
Overprotective	You become very cautious. You are inhibited participating in sports and physical activities.	You are careless, reckless, and don't pay attention to danger. You use poor judgment about taking risks.	You are very restrictive towards others, especially your children. You see danger everywhere.
Underprotective	You take unnecessary chances and let yourself become exposed to danger. You don't notice the usual warning signs of trouble.	You become overly cautious and can't have fun easily. You are overly alert to possible trouble in most situations.	With your children and others, you tend to ignore signs of danger and allow others to endanger themselves.
Overly righteous and disdainful of others	You highlight your moral failings. You may get in trouble with the authorities.	You parade your moral virtues.	You are disdainful of and gloat about faults in others. You search them out.
Amoral or sociopathic	You have trouble following the rules and doing the right thing.	You insist on honesty in all your dealings and are intolerant of crooks and cheaters.	You use people and get what you want whatever the means.

Controlling and Authoritarian Parents or Siblings

A parent or sibling who is overbearing, authoritarian, and controlling will make us feel obligated to give in and to submit. What prevents us from being independent is that our parent or sibling experiences any act of independence on our part as willful, offensive, and threatening behavior.

Your mind-set might be "Standing up for myself makes my father furious. I'd better be accommodating and just do what he wants. But giving in is humiliating, so I'll just pretend to go along, and resist and be stubborn whenever I can."

As an adult, fearing that you might become too accommodating and submissive if you were emotionally close to your spouse could cause you to continually argue or be contrary as a way of proving your independence.

One of my clients, Will, was a wealthy businessman. Will resisted almost all requests of him by his wife Dorothy. He agitated and provoked her by saying no whenever she asked for something or suggested anything. This occurred whether the suggestion was important or meaningless. No matter what, Will said no. Why did he do this?

Will had been strongly sensitized to giving in to others by a deadly combination of parental traits. His father, authoritarian and pompous, required his son to accept his point of view and give in to his orders. His father would pout and act angry if his son didn't accommodate him. This was experienced by Will to mean that his father was weak and always needed to be in charge or to be right. He complied with this so that his father could maintain his position of authority and feel important.

His mother, on the other hand, treated Will as her confidant and companion in order to compensate for her husband's disinterest in her, which she confided to her son. This caused Will to feel obligated to honor her requests, cheer her up, and spend time with her so that she wouldn't be so lonely and unhappy.

Will's mind-set was "Doing what makes me happy makes my parents unhappy." The shorthand version of this, which became encoded in his mind, was the commandment "Accommodation is good."

When Will came in for therapy, his complaint was that he and his wife fought all the time, and that he couldn't stand her because she was too demanding and critical of him. He had no awareness that his problem with her was mainly due to his inability to say yes, even when he wanted to. The commandment "Accommodation is good" had become so entrenched in Will's mind that any request from his wife was experienced by him as dangerous.

Any desire expressed by his wife, no matter how delicately or diplomatically presented, was experienced by Will as a demand to submit. Since both he and his wife were independently wealthy, it was ironic that he would resist any of her suggestions that they spend money, no matter how large or small the sum involved.

Nor was the problem confined to Will's marriage. As you might expect, every relationship caused him to worry about being trapped into serving the other person. Why wouldn't it? He had been used and dominated by both of his parents for years.

When Will became aware of the historical source of his problem, a light came on. He began to realize that he equated reasonable requests with the unpleasant demands of his parents, and as a result was unable to properly assess his wife's requests and suggestions. As a result, he started to reassess his responses to his wife. What followed was an increasing comfort with saying no to her when he meant it, and saying yes when that was a more appropriate response. The fighting between them began to diminish. Disagreements now took on new meaning for Will. They didn't have to just serve the purpose of fighting against giving in. Now they could also reflect his actual point of view.

In another case where submitting to a parent was the primary problem, a financial planner named Sherman, unlike Will, didn't rebel and fight but gave in to almost all requests of him by his friends and clients. He accommodated.

Sherman was in his early forties when he first came for therapy. He complained that in his business dealings he had difficulty saying no to financial requests that he objected to. When clients asked that he lend them money, he would usually comply but later resent it. His initial goal in therapy was to be able to refuse to lend money when he wanted to.

At the same time, Sherman was in the throes of his first serious relationship. This should have been a positive experience but instead was very threatening to him. I wasn't surprised to learn that his mother had totally controlled and dominated him, requiring him to be overly compliant to her wishes. A close relationship with a woman was, therefore, very frightening to him.

When he learned that he was afraid to hurt or disappoint people by saying no to their requests of him, Sherman began to feel more comfortable refusing them. After he became more successful saying no to people, he began to recall instances of how his mother had dominated him. That led him to have better understanding of his fear of being controlled when he began to feel emotionally involved with a woman.

If you have suffered as Will and Sherman did, you probably also act in ways you hate. You may be spineless, self-sacrificing, depressed, or dissatisfied, as Sherman was, and find you are having unproductive relationships because of your destructive past experiences and the mind-sets that may have resulted from them.

If you are like Will, you may be stubborn and provocative as a result of rebelling against your past. Your current relationships can thus become haunted by the ghosts of pain from past relationships. These overlay the substance of your life, obscuring the actual problem.

If you can illuminate these ghosts with the spotlight of understanding, they will recede into their true place in the past. They will lose their power over you because you can use your knowledge to counter their self-destructive effects. But if they remain hidden, they will dictate to you that to be yourself, or the best you can be, will hurt your parents or siblings. Like a primitive tribe that feels it has to placate an offended god through self-sacrificing behaviors, you can ruin your life in an attempt to placate the gods of your childhood: your parents.

Since they are hidden, your childhood mind-sets can cause you to distort your expectations of future relationships and therefore to act inappropriately as an adult. They may also keep you from enjoying your accomplishments.

Rejecting Parents and Siblings

A parent or sibling who is rejecting toward you makes it difficult for you to feel close to him or her or to anyone else. The mind-set you develop might be "Trying to be close to my mother (father) burdens and upsets her; therefore, I won't demand attention or affection from her."

The belief that you hurt your mother by trying to be close to her keeps you at a distance from her and also causes you to feel guilty for wanting to be close. Eventually, you may assume that all other people are the same as your mother, causing you to keep your distance from them as well.

In order to not feel guilty, you may transform your need for closeness and affection into the mind-set "Independence is good," then automatically change your behavior in response to this belief. As a result, you could easily suppress your need for emotional response and become overly self-reliant in order to not risk being a burden to anyone. Your experience was that desiring closeness with your mother led to rejection. Therefore, you worry that if you promote close or intimate relationships with other people, they will be burdened and you will be rejected.

Later in life, to protect yourself from rejection, you might resist verbalizing your desires, complaints, or problems because you may feel these will burden your partner, friends, coworkers, and even your children.

If instead you rebelled against being rejected by your mother, you might become insistent on having your demands met or act very provocatively until you were responded to. This rebellious response could cause you to feel guilty for burdening or provoking your parent and cause you to have self-critical thoughts like "I'm too needy." If your guilt feelings become too intense, you might revert to accommodating behavior again.

As we have discussed, another way you might avoid the awareness of unpleasant memories of rejection is to do to others what was done to you. You may develop a rejecting attitude yourself and be cold to your spouse, children, and others when they attempt to be close to you. You will probably be perfectly aware that being cold and rejecting towards your spouse and children is hurtful and creates distance between you. But you may be compelled to act this way because it helps you to suppress your memories of how you were rejected as a child by your parents.

In the process of acting rejecting toward your children, you will feel dissatisfied when your children keep their distance from you. This will serve as your punishment for having burdened your mother by trying to be close to her.

I treated a woman named Lydia who complained bitterly about being mistreated in practically every situation of her life. In her childhood she had suffered from severe rejection from her mother, who was cruel and cold to her. What was significant was how Lydia interpreted her mother's coldness. Her mind-set was that her mother's motivations were based on fear that Lydia would interfere with her mother's need to be the center of attention, especially with her brother and father. Whenever Lydia made attempts to be close to her brother or father, her mother would become very critical and reject her.

In response to this, Lydia was troubled whenever she interacted with her brother or father. She always felt as though they were mistreating her, even when they were treating her properly. This reaction was an unconscious attempt to accommodate to her sense of guilt towards her mother. That is, Lydia felt that if she was made unhappy by her brother and father, her mother would stop rejecting her. Conversely, if her relationships with them were happy, this would cause her mother to act cruelly towards her. Although it was true that her brother and father failed her in certain ways, she overreacted to their behavior in order to placate her mother. Lydia had no idea that her sense of victimization was caused by her own psyche.

The other response Lydia had to her mother's rejection of her was to rebelliously become very insistent on getting attention, no matter how inappropriately she had to act. Ironically, this put people off, thereby compounding her sense of rejection.

In her therapy, as Lydia became aware of the nature of the forces compelling her negativity, she became both relieved and less anxious. The anxiety was based on feeling undeserving of a non-victim status in life. This reflected her haunting memories of her mother not wanting her to be happy. Understanding this enabled her to realize what her mind-sets were and how they interfered with her benefiting from therapy. The idea that she should be happy was contrary to Lydia's mind-set. She gradually became freer and learned to overcome her suffering as she integrated this knowledge.

Possessive Parents or Siblings

Family members like these want you to be wholly focused on or primarily involved with them. This will make you feel guilty about being close with others, and in this way compromise your independence.

The following mind-set is a common one in this situation: "If I have lots of friends, find other people interesting, or enjoy myself away from home, my parent will feel hurt because I am disloyal to him or her. Therefore, I should avoid or be cautious about getting involved with new people and situations." Some children experience discomfort about the pleasure they experience when they leave home to go away to summer camp or college. They may feel guilty towards one or both parents about enjoying being on their own. When the guilt is more pronounced it can lead to a school phobia. The child's fear of going to school reflects his or her underlying worry about upsetting a parent as a result of enjoying new relationships at school.

The positive commandment that results from this mind-set is "Loyalty is best." As a result of this, you could easily become shy, be isolated from people, fear getting trapped by involvements, and feel that life is not fun. You might notice that whenever you do involve yourself with others, you become over-solicitous of them as you did with your mother. In response to this behavior, people may see you as very sensitive. But underneath, you will hate yourself for being so loyal. A relationship will be an enormous burden to you because you will feel that you have to be devoted (accommodate) to the other person at the expense of your independence and relationships with others.

On the other hand, in order to protect yourself from the burden and obligation of always pleasing others, you could easily rebel. You might become overly focused on your own interests and ignore what the other person wants. Then, ironically, you may be thought of as self-centered!

Finally, if you were to do to others what was done to you, you might suffocate your loved ones emotionally and feel irrationally jealous whenever attention was paid to others.

A case in point is the story of Ronald, a dynamic businessman. Ronald struggled all his life against the excessive demands of his mother. She was possessive of him and experienced her main fulfillment in life through his accomplishments and her relationship with him. He felt he was just an object to serve her needs. He felt cheated.

All good mothers care for their children, but Ronald's mother loved him and needed him too much, causing him to feel overly responsible for her well-being. He was playing out his life according to the commandment "Mother comes first," which he then generalized to everyone. His problem was that his mind-set did not include taking care of himself.

You might wonder, "What about his father? What was he doing all this time?" Ronald's father was needy, weak, and passive. This made him unable to model for his son how to resist his mother.

In response to his mother's need to be primary in Ronald's life, he had trouble leaving her to go to school at age five. For most of his first year in kindergarten, he vomited every day on the way to school. This physical response was caused by his worry that his mother would be upset that he was away from her and that he might enjoy it.

When he finally left home and an excellent job on the East Coast to come to California at the age of twenty-six, Ronald experienced chest pains after crossing the Mississippi River. In retrospect, he attributed this to the guilt he felt over leaving his mother, knowing that once he was past the midpoint of his trip, there was no turning back. Although he was twenty-six years old, he reacted physically just as he had at the age of five when he first separated from his mother. Ronald didn't realize that subconsciously he believed he was hurting his mother by looking forward to leaving her behind.

Similarly, as an adult, every time Ronald tried to advance his interests, he experienced strong guilt feelings about rejecting and hurting others, for which he would atone by experiencing physical symptoms. For instance, when he left a business partner to start his own firm, he developed a severe case of pneumonia.

When occasionally he rebelled against the requirements of his "Others come first" mind-set, Ronald went to the other extreme and became overly focused on his own interests to the exclusion of others. This made him appear to his wife (and others) as extremely self-centered, when in fact he was struggling to protect and preserve his own well-being in the face of a very self-centered mother. Ronald was afraid of being sucked into the orbit of others, as he had been with his mother. Like a swimmer frantically using exaggerated strokes out of fear of being pulled under by a nearby swimmer, Ronald kept his emotional distance from others.

In another interesting case, a man named Henry also experienced the oppression of a female relative. When he was a child, his grandmother, who lived with his family, adored him, babied him, and experienced her main fulfillment in life through her relationship with him. The mind-set he unconsciously developed was that "Grandmother needs to mother me in order to be happy." Until the age of fourteen, when she died, he frequently wet his bed at night so that his grandmother could come into his room, change his sheets, and comfort him.

In Henry's unconscious mind, wetting his bed reassured his grandmother that he was still her baby, so that she could fulfill her maternal role. Growing up would deprive her of the opportunity to mother him and cause him to feel guilty towards her. Once she died, the symptom disappeared.

Competitive and Self-Centered Parents or Siblings

This type of parent or sibling insists that their interests always come first. As we've discussed earlier, this attitude makes it difficult for you to feel good about getting attention, success, and status for yourself. In response to the mind-set "Being the center of attention hurts my father, mother, or sibling, so I'd better stay in the background and avoid recognition and success," you might develop the internal commandment "Modesty is good."

A doctor named Robert responded to such a commandment. He felt that he was a fraud whenever he made a presentation, in spite of being considered an expert in his field. His father was a businessman who compensated for feeling inadequate by putting other people down and never giving them credit for their accomplishments. None of his criticisms of others, however, ever applied to himself.

This father avoided acknowledging his son's accomplishments, causing Robert to unconsciously conclude that his father would be threatened by his achievements. As a result, instead of thinking highly of himself, Robert felt that he was a fraud in order to maintain his father's false sense of esteem.

Another client, Dan, was a lawyer with a similar mind-set. He rarely spoke up to challenge his father's opinions. He stayed in the background at school and as an adult was passive at his job. Dan hated himself for holding back in situations where he knew he could excel, but he avoided speaking up. In the process, he prevented himself from being noticed and therefore promoted. Dan's unconscious motive, like Robert's, was to preserve his father's self-esteem by being inferior.

Had Dan rebelled against his father's treatment of him, he might have insisted on being recognized for his accomplishments, refusing to acknowledge or give credit to others.

There were also instances in Dan's social life in which he behaved towards others the way his father did with him. He would put them down and make himself the center of attention. This served to help him forget that he had been treated the same way during his childhood.

The following story is another illustration how people diminish their accomplishments in response to their destructive mind-sets.

Eric, a client who had always achieved more than his father, complained after each success instead of celebrating it. He felt that his success was spoiling his father's happiness, so he had to spoil his own. On one occasion, after landing a big account, Eric got drunk, presumably to celebrate his success. He followed this by getting into a fight with a colleague, which undermined his accomplishment.

If your parent was overprotective of a weak sister or brother, he or she might have communicated to you that you should not do too well for the sake of your sibling's self-esteem. You might have developed the mind-set "If I stand out in school or sports, my brother or sister will feel diminished by comparison with me and will look bad to my parents." As a result, as an adult you may find yourself unable to succeed in spite of your talent (see the story of Fred, Chapter Four).

If your father competed with you to be the most-liked person in the family, to prevent him from feeling less popular you might have developed the thought "I'd better keep myself uninteresting so my father won't feel threatened." Without recognizing the mind-set at work, you would only have been aware of your dissatisfaction with your lack of social success.

If you notice that, as a boy, being special to your mother makes your father act competitively with you, you are likely to think, "If I'm liked by my mother, my father will feel slighted or rejected. Therefore, I should keep my distance from her." As an adult, you may generalize this to all situations, being aware only that you hate yourself for being unable to pursue or enjoy satisfying relationships with the opposite sex.

Depressed and Needy Parents or Siblings

Needy parents or siblings might make you feel that it was wrong to feel happy or might make you feel obligated to rescue them. Remember the case of Henry, who suffered bed wetting until his teenage years as a result of asking himself, "How can I be happy when Grandmother is suffering?" His belief was, "She needs me, so I'd better be there for her and not think of myself." Notice that there are some similarities between depressed or needy parents and/or siblings and possessive ones. Both kinds of family members are needy, but depressed family members bring the added burden of making a child feel that being happy is wrong.

A man named Jack came to me with the complaint that he was unable to feel happy. He couldn't understand why. The reason became apparent as he described how accommodating to his depressed, widowed mother had negatively impacted his adult life. His mother's involvement with life revolved solely around her son. She was so needy and depressed that Jack felt he ought to be devoted to fulfilling her pursuit of gratification. This required him to ignore his needs and become overly sensitive to and worried about her feelings. He believed that his happiness would cause her to suffer depression and neediness. What could he do? Unconsciously, Jack reasoned that he was responsible for his mother's depression. While her attachment to him gave meaning to her life and relieved her sense of despair and worthlessness, it diminished him.

In time, this mind-set was generalized to other people, causing Jack to feel stressed in almost every relationship in which someone depended on him or where he had authority over them. His stress was caused by the tension between fulfilling the needs of others and neglecting his own.

When dating women, Jack unconsciously rebelled against the obligation he felt to take care of them by keeping his emotional distance from them and thereby communicating that he was unavailable. When he took care of himself, on the other hand, he felt guilty and became depressed. This was payment in kind based on erroneously believing that caring for himself caused his girlfriend (his mother) to become depressed.

This pattern of thought interfered with making choices in his life. Jack felt it was wrong to consider his own interests. One area in which this became evident was his decision about the right career to pursue.

Similarly, when his job required him to assert his authority, Jack felt great stress because he couldn't comfortably exercise his personal power. His mind-set caused him to unconsciously worry that he was causing others distress in this situation. As in the experiences he had with his mother, he was too sensitive to hurting people by making decisions that weren't sympathetic enough to their interests. The outcome was that Jack lived with a sense of quiet resignation and underlying frustration.

On the other hand, in a job where his decision making was more limited, he felt resentful that his abilities were not appreciated. You can see how Jack's destructive mind-set prevented him from finding a comfortable niche for himself.

An interesting point was the way he treated me. At times he complained and acted depressed in his therapy, the way his mother had behaved with him. This is an example of the client doing to the therapist what was done to him. Jack was hoping that I would be less worried about his unhappiness than he was about his mother's. It was his unconscious attempt to learn, by watching me, how to be less sensitive to unhappy people. In this way he could feel freer to fulfill his own needs.

Parents or Siblings Who Live Through Your Accomplishments

These parents or siblings can provoke you to develop mind-sets that pressure you to achieve success and perfection in order to not disappoint them. You may feel worried about falling short of their high expectations of you, and as a result you will experience anxiety when you have to perform in competitive sports, school exams, and your job. Ironically, this anxiety will actually interfere with achieving the perfection your parents or siblings require. People with this mind-set are usually extremely critical of themselves when they don't win or perform well, but they are not always satisfied when they do well.

One very successful but driven businessman was motivated by striving for perfection. He complained to me that he couldn't stand admiration from others because he felt there would then be greater expectations of him to perform at even higher levels.

When you are motivated by this mind-set, nothing you do is ever good enough because you unconsciously worry that your parents' or siblings' well-being depends on your achievements. Everyone is familiar with the parent who is never satisfied with his or her child's grades, no matter how good they are. The same parent may express dissatisfaction with the child's performance in most other areas of life. If you accommodate to these parental expectations, you may find yourself compulsively driven to achieve, no matter the cost to you.

Your attempts to relax via hobbies and recreational sports may be frustrated as you apply the same standards of perfection to them. One very accomplished company president took up golf for relaxation, but much to his dismay, he found himself exasperated about his inability to meet his standards of perfection.

Another man, named James, had been a brilliant student all his life, but dropped out of law school as an act of rebellion against his mother's excessive standards of perfection. He felt that he had been performing for her his whole life without considering what was best for him. He realized that he was going to law school to please his mother rather than himself. He dropped out in protest, hoping that his mother would accept him as he was. Leaving school made James experience profound guilt for disappointing his mother's grand expectations for his future. Therefore, he had to suffer and become depressed as payment for his feelings of guilt instead of enjoying his new lifestyle. This was reinforced by his mother's continual expressions of great dismay over his decision.

In his therapy with me, James continued to rebel against meeting the expectations of others. He frustrated whatever expectations he thought I had of him, while hoping I would not be disappointed with him as his mother had been.

For example, he would arrive late for his therapy sessions. Once he had arrived, he would refuse to talk. Because I refused to allow his behavior to provoke me, he became less hostile toward therapy and eventually came to see how his mind-set had caused him to take a rebellious path in life. Eventually, James developed a greater awareness about what he wanted for himself. He changed his life accordingly and pursued his true interests.

If you are a person with the mind-set that you are obliged to fulfill your parents' need to live through your accomplishments, you will be susceptible to guilt feelings for disappointing them. In response to this sense of guilt, you will feel that you deserve to be disappointed in the same way with your own children and others as punishment.

Parents or Siblings Who Demand Loyalty

Parents and siblings who make these demands are similar to possessive family members. The parent or sibling who demands loyalty, however, may not necessarily also require a smothering closeness, although they do expect loyalty to specific values and a certain lifestyle. If the child chooses to develop an interest in the wrong people, religious and political beliefs, and traditions, the parent or sibling will act betrayed, causing the child to feel guilty, as in the story of Alice in Chapter Two.

An adult who was raised in this situation might wonder why he or she inexplicably provokes fights with intimates, not realizing that this behavior is the result of guilt feelings. If, for example, you became involved with people your parents disapprove of

(for reasons of race, religion, or social or econom[
might fight with these people in order to relieve t[
ings caused by your disloyalty. In other words, fath[
does know best. You might also fear intimacy, for f[
ing in new relationships the enslavement and restrictions that
you felt with your parents or siblings.

A client named Anne had severe problems with men, which
stemmed from loyalty issues with her parents. They had incul-
cated in their daughter their very strongly held beliefs that she
should only become involved with wealthy men of high social
class. Anne complied by marrying a man who met their standards but not her own. She felt like a puppet without autonomy.
This caused her to unconsciously experience deep resentment,
which led to chronic dissatisfaction, fights with her husband,
and a divorce.

In another important relationship later on, with a man she
liked, Anne also complained of having many fights and disagreements. This time her dissatisfaction was the result of
unconscious guilt caused by feeling disloyal to her parents, who
would have strongly disapproved of this man. Until she began
to understand her hidden mind-set, Anne was unable to experience happiness with either a man her parents preferred, or one
that she did. She was unable escape from the pain of disloyalty
and guilt on the one hand, and accommodation and resentment
on the other.

A professional man named Chris, who was adopted when he
was two, developed a strong sense of loyalty to the parents who
rescued him. His sense of obligation and loyalty was intensified by
his mother, who expected appreciation for what she had done on
his behalf. She manipulated Chris to feel this way by acting hurt
if he wasn't attentive to her or didn't adhere to her values.

When Chris decided to move away to complete his post-
graduate training, his mother complained and became very upset that he hadn't considered a training program closer to where
she lived. This intensified his sense of guilt toward her. He wondered, "Am I being disloyal for not considering my mother's desire that I be close by?"

You would think that this man would avoid any relationships with other women. But instead, he came for therapy

because of a depression he experienced after his girlfriend had rejected him. He had unconsciously developed a relationship with a woman who was rejecting in order to punish himself for rejecting his mother.

Chris might have continued getting involved with rejecting women in order to demonstrate his loyalty to his mother and to also pay for his crime of disloyalty. If so, he would have gone through life hating himself for selecting women who didn't truly care for him. This is one example of why, because of a hidden mind-set, we have difficulty learning from our bad experiences.

Anna, another client, was unable to hire a nurse to help with the care of her sick father, until she discovered in her therapy that her mind-set required her to be overly devoted to him, usually at great expense to herself.

If, like Chris's mother, your parents want you to admire and appreciate what they have done for you, they may act hurt if you speak highly of your experiences with other adults. This might inhibit you from developing experiences with people whom you admire more than your parents.

Everyone is familiar with parents who are terribly disturbed if their children marry outside their religion, race, or economic class. Before the mid-twentieth century, with all of its mobility and its social, economic, and educational possibilities, people had fewer opportunities to deviate from their family values and traditions. People's futures were predetermined by their economic class. Young women automatically married and had children. Young men automatically followed in their father's trade and lived their lives defined by the values of their parents' class. Therefore, there was probably less guilt about surpassing one's parents and deviating from their expectations.

In the movie *The Bronx Tale,* Robert DeNiro plays the role of a bus driver who is hard working, honest, and loyal to his wife. However, in his son's eyes, he seems weak compared to the local Mafia hood, who has money, power, and glamour.

The Mafia boss and the boy take a liking to each other, causing the son to feel guilty toward his father. DeNiro's character is hurt by and resentful of his son's greater admiration for the Mafia boss. Wanting to move beyond his father's limited world causes the son to feel guilty for being disloyal to his father and his father's values.

Weak or Ineffectual Parents or Siblings

Such parents and siblings make you worry about their inability to set limits, to take care of themselves, or to get what they want. This interferes with your own ability to become assertive and leads to two possible mind-sets. The first is "If I am strong and stand up for my opinions, or get what I want, my mother or father will cave in, become agitated, or look forlorn. Therefore, I'd better act meek, not show that I can get what I want, and keep my opinions to myself."

The other mind-set is "I may get out of control, since my parent is too weak to set limits; therefore, I'd better control myself."

What are the outcomes of these two mind-sets?

If you accommodate to a parent who is too controlling and powerful, you could overrespect authority, becoming conservative and unspontaneous. If acting strong is seen as bad, weakness becomes a virtue. When a child has a parent who is weak and ineffectual, the child may fear getting out of control and trampling on the parent. Therefore, the child develops an exaggerated sense of his or her power, which must be restrained. Thus, weakness becomes a virtue again.

This way of thinking can surface in disagreements with a weak parent who might give in or become overly emotional. If you feel that your parent's weakness is a result of your strength, you will probably feel obligated to punish yourself by acting weak as well. *This outcome demonstrates that a child's beliefs about hurting a parent are primary.*

You might think that when parents act blustery, self-centered, and opinionated, children would see this as strength. But that contradicts how, as children, we actually see our parents. Instead, we perceive their behavior as a cover for inadequacy and weakness because it reveals to us that they are fragile, can't tolerate disagreements, or allow someone else to be right. Therefore, we protect our parents from feeling inadequate by keeping ourselves unassertive. That is what causes us to keep ourselves weak.

Raymond is an example of a man who had to restrain his strength in the face of weakness. This talented administrator had one sibling with a physical disability and another who performed in life at a much lower level than Raymond.

In response to this situation, Raymond quelled his competitive urges. This inability to compete showed up in his tennis game. (Well, what weakness doesn't?) Raymond consistently lost at tennis to people with weaker skills and became totally exasperated with himself. He only felt comfortable playing well against stronger opponents. Unconsciously, he was trying to protect people who were weak (sibling substitutes) from experiencing weakness in comparison with his strength. When he got ahead in a match, he would usually allow some distraction to interfere with his success.

Raymond also diminished his potential success in other areas of his life. He had the mind-set "It is upsetting to my siblings that I am admired so much by my family. In comparison, my parents are very worried about them. Therefore, I ought to lessen my opportunities for glory, so they will look more competent and feel more worthwhile." Raymond hated himself for not performing up to his potential in life, and when he did well, he would downplay his accomplishments or present himself in a very understated way. In other words, he tried to appear weaker than he was. He would then resent not receiving admiration.

Jane was an overweight nurse whose mother had a poor relationship with Jane's father. This was in contrast with the father's adoration of Jane. The discrepancy caused Jane to feel sorry for her mother.

Jane perceived that her mother's inability to assert herself and promote a worthwhile relationship with her father was due to passivity and weakness. She was afraid that her good relationship with her father would somehow hurt her weak and unhappy mother. Therefore, Jane developed the mind-set that because she was stronger and more desirable than her mother, she was therefore responsible for her mother being displaced and unhappy. (This is very similar to how stronger siblings feel about the weaker ones they dominate. They often feel responsible when the weaker siblings develop problems.)

Jane was unable to see that her mother's weakness and unhappiness with her father was independent of Jane's connection with him. This caused her to feel guilty. In order to assuage her feelings of guilt, she became overweight in order to keep men away. She was not aware of how her mind-set affected her inability to lose weight.

Another client named Maxine was a married artist with a similar problem. Maxine made herself emotionally unavailable to men. Whereas Jane made herself physically unattractive, Maxine's guilt compelled her to be cold and distant.

She started behaving this way with her father, hoping that he would distance himself from her and instead pay more attention to her unhappy mother. Because Maxine thought her mother's plight resulted from her father's interest in her, she felt undeserving of anything better from her own husband. She kept him away by acting cold, too.

Remember the comedian in *Mr. Saturday Night,* who believed that his success hurt his weak, ineffectual brother? He not only diminished his opportunities to achieve, but when he did achieve he couldn't enjoy it. His severe sense of guilt robbed him of the ability to be happy.

COMPETITION AND WEAKNESS

What is it that causes guilt in competing with others? It's the belief that someone has been hurt and it's your fault. Winning or losing isn't the heart of the issue; it's more a matter of assessing yourself and others as "winners" or "losers."

Ecologically speaking, competition exists in every relationship we have in the world. We compete with the rest of creation for our place on earth. How well we compete determines whether we will live, reproduce, and pass on our genes to succeeding generations.

Competition in familial relationships is a natural offshoot of this truth. Dominance and submission, rivalry and cooperation, opposition and participation are all aspects of competition within the context of family. Our position in our family and our sense of self-worth are caught up in this issue. But since we develop an understanding of these things when we are quite young, there has to be an internal system of assessment to help us.

The internal system that helps us is the ability to perceive whether the reaction of our opponent results from a position of strength or a position of weakness. So, how well we oppose someone is largely determined by our guilt or the lack of it in competing.

Wanting to defeat an opponent doesn't necessarily make us feel guilty enough to act in ways that are self-defeating. We don't always have to hold back our successes or diminish ourselves. However, if your opponent is truly weak, competition will seem unfair. A bad loser may try to take advantage of this truth by communicating to you that he or she is weak, hurt, and diminished by the experience of losing. This may make you feel sorry for that person and guilty for causing him or her pain. This spoils your sense of accomplishment and can prevent you from competing successfully.

Contrast this with someone who, in losing graciously, makes it possible for you to enjoy your victory without feeling guilty. He or she obviously enjoyed the competition and didn't feel diminished by losing.

There is more to competition than what appears on the surface! Remember, your feelings of self-worth are wrapped up in how you compete in general. Is your competitor truly weak, fragile, threatened, and vulnerable? If so, will you feel guilty in competing with that person? Or is that person confident, strong, and self-sufficient in his or her dealings with you? If so, even if you easily best your competitor, the experience won't diminish either of you and shouldn't cause you guilt.

Just as we can usually gauge the strength of our competitors, as children we are also able to perceive the true nature of our parents and siblings. We know unconsciously whether our parent or sibling is relating to us from a position of strength or weakness. Thus, if we see a loved one hurt by our behavior, we will usually inhibit ourselves even at the expense of our best interests.

If you are a parent with a child of the same sex, you can verify this by watching this child compete with you for the affection of your spouse. If you are a male and your son, age four to seven, says he wants you to go away so he can marry Mommy, you can think of it as charming and amusing behavior or as threatening. The former response will help the child to feel confident about competing because he perceives your strength. The latter may have a disturbing effect on him. Your reaction will therefore cause your son to perceive you as either strong or weak.

Parents Who Abuse Alcohol or Drugs

Parents with alcohol and drug problems who are unpredictable, volatile, or violent can cause extreme anxiety in their children. One of my clients, a lawyer named Rose, came to me for help because of powerful feelings of anxiety that were aroused in her whenever she had to confront or disagree with someone. This profoundly affected her ability to function as a lawyer. The problem was caused by her experiences with her alcoholic father, who exploded in violent rages if he was confronted when intoxicated.

Rose was not aware that being excessively vigilant or anxious was connected to her childhood fears that something terrible might happen when her father became drunk. As she became more aware of the source of her difficulty in handling disagreements, she became more effective at work. She realized that she didn't have to feel guilty if someone became upset because of her point of view.

In response to such a parent, a child will not only develop heightened vigilance and worry about people losing control, but he or she may be overly worried about causing someone to explode or act erratically. A client named Doris was profoundly affected by the violence of her unpredictable alcoholic parents. Because she had the belief that many of their drunken brawls revolved around her, she went out of her way to placate both parents at great expense to herself. This carried over to her adult life, when she was beloved by many for being so caring and attentive (an outgrowth of placating her parents). However, she exhausted herself in the process and developed powerful hidden resentments that led to physical ailments.

Doris's vigilance showed up in her relationship with her husband. One example of this was her inability to tolerate the slightest change in his mood if he drank a beer. She had an exaggerated fear that this was a prelude to his becoming out of control like her parents. She not only reacted angrily to her husband when he drank, but she avoided all parties where either drugs or alcohol were used.

In rebellion against being so vigilant in her childhood, Doris was in danger of becoming totally negative and unresponsive towards people who were not fully in control of themselves. She did not identify with her parents and become unpredictable or a drinker like them; instead she went to the opposite extreme of becoming utterly reliable and steady.

Critical Parents or Siblings

Family members may repeatedly find fault with one or more of your behaviors, characteristics, or thoughts. Of course, the crucial issue as to how the criticism affects you is what you decide is the reason for it and whether it's something you can change or not.

If you feel the criticism is for something you can't change, such as your looks or the fact that you were an unwanted child, you will have more difficulty dealing with it. You will be left feeling unworthy because there is something wrong with you that you can never fix. Closely akin to this is a general tone of criticism for everything you do. Obviously, the more difficult it is to perceive what you have done wrong, the more difficult it is to make changes in your behavior to ease the situation.

General criticism leads to poor self-esteem and excessive self-blame: "Everything I do is wrong. I'm no good. If Father wanted me to do well, he wouldn't criticize me. So, why do well?"

Other types of criticisms will also cause you to behave in ways you hate as an adult. If, for example, you are criticized for being independent, you may inhibit your autonomy or quest for freedom and reassure your parents by asking them for advice and guidance. You may then, later on, hate yourself for being a follower rather than a leader.

If you feel you are being put down because of your charm and popularity, you may inhibit those qualities and hate yourself for being a shy and retiring person.

If you feel the criticism is based on your lack of achievement, you may be afraid to fail. Performance anxiety when you take exams or have to perform in other ways may paralyze you. This, of course, will interfere with your ability to do well and cause you to disappoint your parents even more. Now you will feel pressured to do better the next time, intensifying your anxiety. This behavior pattern could remain with you all your life and create unnecessary difficulties for you when you have to perform in school, in sports, and at work.

What if you rebelled against your critical parent? You might end up denying that anything is ever your fault. You might be unable to ever accept any constructive criticism, suggestions, or recommendations. This would greatly hamper your success in relationships with others.

To avoid remembering how painful your parents' criticism was for you, you might easily be critical with your children. As a result, in spite of your desire to not be like your parents, you will have assumed their behavior and hate yourself for it.

Unprotective Parents

Parents who are unprotective create another set of problems. When you accommodate to a parent who is unprotective of you with regard to perilous situations, or who in fact promotes your exposure to risk, you will probably have difficulty noticing the usual warning signs of danger and protecting yourself. You may believe your parent wants you to suffer a harmful fate, and therefore you may feel that it is wrong to protect yourself. One woman who had such a mother remembered taking incredible risks when hitchhiking as a teenager. She would get into cars with seedy and potentially dangerous men.

A common but complicated situation arises in families where there is sexual molestation. If the mother is told about it, or knows about it but does nothing to protect her daughter, the daughter will feel betrayed and unprotected. She may be afraid to complain, in order to protect her mother from having to confront the unpleasant truth about her father.

One client, named Elaine, had a mother who couldn't protect her from her father. She concluded that her mother was so weak that she needed to be protected by her daughter. So she quietly submitted to his abuse. Standing up for herself and protesting against being a victim was very difficult for Elaine because her destructive mind-set made her feel guilty: "If I stand up for my interests, my mother will suffer." Either she submitted, she thought, or her mother would suffer violent abuse from her father.

The other way Elaine protected her mother was to blame herself for the molestation. Just as she let her mother off the hook in childhood, in later life she overlooked the deficiencies of others.

In other cases, where the mother strongly confronts her husband or leaves the marriage in order to protect her daughter, the daughter will admire her mother's strength. However, if the mother remains unhappy after the divorce, or avoids getting involved with men, the daughter may actually feel guilty for contributing to the breakup of her mother's marriage. That guilt can lead to self-destructive relationships with men as penance.

On the other hand, if you rebel against an un-protective parent, you may become overly cautious and alert to trouble everywhere and at all times. You may never be able to relax.

Parents Who Are Overprotective

These parents are also damaging to children. For a review of this situation, look back at Chapter Five and the case of Tina.

Summary

As a child, you have three major choices in dealing with specific deficiencies in your parents and siblings.

First, you can hold yourself back in order to accommodate to and get along with your parents and siblings. Inhibiting your behavior helps you feel that you have not hurt them. If your parents or siblings are domineering, you may become submissive and obedient. If they are possessive, you may stay close to them. In any case, you are bound to harbor some resentment about compromising your development, whether you are aware of it or not.

Second, you can rebel against your family's bad behavior and hope they get the message from your rebellion that their behavior is detrimental to you and should stop. If your parents or siblings are domineering, you may become overtly defiant and uncooperative, or more quietly defiant in a passive-aggressive way. If your parents or siblings are possessive, you may stay distant from them and spitefully become overly involved with others. However, you will probably experience guilt by doing so, because you will feel that your family is hurt or provoked by your rebellion.

These rebellious guilt feelings can be relieved by again becoming accommodating to your parent or sibling, by self-destructive acts that serve as penance, by developing new moral commandments (Chapter Six) and self-critical thoughts, and by becoming like the parents you believed you hurt.

Third, you may become like your parents and siblings even when you'd prefer not to, then behave the same way towards your spouse, your children, and others. Being the doer instead of the receiver of bad treatment helps you forget that you were hurt by your family and as a result held yourself back. Because you blame yourself for their faults, you feel you deserve to have the same faults yourself. Thus, you become like the parents or siblings you vowed never to be like. If you thought you were responsible for your parent acting domineering or possessive, you may feel you deserve to also be domineering or possessive with your children and others.

In addition to behavior you hate, you may also have thoughts that you hate. You may wonder how this comes about. In the accompanying chart, How Your Parent's Behavior Leads to Thoughts You May Hate (pages 96–97), you will see how this takes place when you accommodate to, rebel against, or become like your parents or siblings.

I would like to explain more about the third column, When You Rebel and Feel Guilty, You May Accept Their Criticisms of You. Feelings of guilt about rebelling cause you to be critical of yourself the way your parent might. For example, an authoritarian parent might say, "You are stubborn as a mule." You might have difficulty disavowing this criticism if you felt that your stubbornness or defiance upset them badly. By comparison, if your parent wasn't hurt by your independence, you wouldn't need to blame yourself.

HOW YOUR PARENT'S BEHAVIOR LEADS TO THOUGHTS YOU MAY HATE

Your Parent or Sibling Is	When You Accommodate You Think	When You Rebel and Feel Guilty, You May Accept Their Criticisms of You	When You Act Like Them You Think
Controlling and authoritarian	"Obedience is good." "Respect your elders." "Parents know best." "God and country above all."	"I'm just stubborn as a mule." "I can't do anything right." "Who do I think I am?"	"Do what I say." "Follow the rules." "You think you know it all."
Rejecting	"Self-reliance is best." "Showing feelings is weak." "Don't depend on others."	"I'm too needy." "I'm too emotional." "I'm just a baby."	"Don't bother me." "Keep your feelings to yourself." "I'm too busy."
Possessive	"Loyalty is good." "Stay away from strangers." "Blood is thicker than water."	"I'm just a flirt." "I'm a traitor." "I don't think of anyone but myself."	"How come you never call or write?" "After all I have done for you." "No one is good enough for you."
Overprotective	"Caution is good." "The world is a dangerous place."	"I'm so careless." "I never watch where I'm going." "I throw caution to the wind."	"You're going to kill yourself." "Watch your step." "Where are you going?"

Competitive and self-centered	"Modesty is good." "Don't be seen, don't be heard." "The meek shall inherit the earth."	"I'm a smart ass." "I'm a show off." "Who do I think I am?" "I'm stupid, ugly, and phony."	"I know best." "I'm great and wonderful." "Look how stupid and disgusting they are." "You think you know it all."
Depressed and needy	"Compassion is best." "Save the poor and downtrodden." "You poor thing." "What can I do to help?"	"I'm too insensitive." "I'm selfish." "I don't think of others."	"Woe is me." "Everything is terrible." "Life is such a problem." "What's the point of living?"
Living through your accomplishments	"Perfection is good." "Succeed at all costs." "My job is never done." "I'll never fail."	"I can't do anything right." "I'm a bum." "I'm a disappointment."	"It's not good enough." "Why can't you get all A's?" "It's not your best."
Unpredictable, uses drugs or alcohol	"Vigilance is best." "Never relax." "I'd better watch my step."	"I'm too blasé." "I have my head in the sand."	"Life is one big party." "Who cares, let's have fun." "Live for the moment."

CHAPTER EIGHT

Double Trouble

I HAVE DESCRIBED HOW THE parent-child dynamic often becomes quite problematic. There is an additional complexity that I call "double trouble." This occurs when, in attempting to accommodate to one parent's peculiarities or shortcomings, you in turn antagonize, provoke, or disappoint the other parent. For example, one parent may feel threatened by their child's success, whereas the other parent needs their child to be successful in order to feel fulfilled. What is a child to do in such a situation?

You are probably already familiar with double troubles that emerge in divorces where the parents compete with each other for the affection of the children. Each parent wants to be preferred as a way of relieving him- or herself of guilt toward the children for being at fault in the family split-up. Or in some instances, one parent wants to get even with the other one by becoming the children's favorite.

This makes it difficult for children to be close to either parent because they fear hurting or betraying the other one. If the children are old enough when the divorce occurs, it may not permanently inhibit their development. But if they are young and more vulnerable, they may learn to inhibit their true feelings toward people, unconsciously fearing that closeness to one person is associated with disappointing someone else.

Success versus Failure

A lawyer named Joel came to me for treatment because of a general sense of anxiety and a specific difficulty in making decisions. His father was a laborer who felt that his status and life accomplishments were beneath his true abilities. As a result of his poor self-esteem and feelings of inadequacy, he would inappropriately boast about himself to inflate his sense of worth. When his son expressed an opinion, his father would put him down, then pontificate on the subject.

Joel's father acted competitively with him and behaved as if he were jealous of the affection his wife gave to his son. In response to this behavior, Joel developed a mind-set that he should be subdued around his father, restrain his pride in his school accomplishments, and keep his opinions to himself.

In contrast, Joel's mother adored and admired her son, and openly talked about how proud of him she felt. She enjoyed his intellectual abilities and academic achievements. Their relationship involved lots of interesting discussions and working together on his homework. Joel felt very encouraged by his mother's admiration, but worried that her self-esteem was tied to his achievements.

The reasons for his anxiety and difficulty making decisions were apparent. When he experienced his mother's pride in him for being bright and accomplished, he felt as if he were threatening his father's self-esteem and causing him to feel jealous. When he accommodated his father by acting subdued and keeping his opinions to himself, Joel disappointed his mother, who enjoyed him when he was lively and interesting to talk to.

Joel was experiencing "double trouble": He was caught in a psychological conflict because of the differing requirements of his parents. In response to this struggle, he developed a strong ambivalence. He went back and forth between shining and being subdued. Every choice had to be judged by whether it hurt his mother or whether it hurt his father. Joel's adult life was characterized by the same indecisiveness.

As a result, he had difficulties asserting himself in his career and pursuing relationships with women. In fact, being successful with women caused him to feel he was simultaneously disappointing both parents. His father was threatened by any success he had in life, so if Joel had a successful relationship with a woman, this would make his father feel jealous. Although his mother was supportive of his accomplishments, Joel believed that he was providing his mother with the companionship she was missing in her marriage. Therefore, he unconsciously believed that if he developed a close relationship with a woman, he would displace his mother and disappoint her.

As you might surmise, Joel's sex life with women was not easy. In order to become aroused and maintain his erection during intercourse, Joel had to have fantasies of his girlfriend having sex with another man. Not only did he tell her about them, but he often insisted that she tell him that she was having enjoyable thoughts of sex with other men. Why did he do this?

The purpose of this was to decrease his guilt towards both parents by assuring them that not only was he an inadequate lover, but that he also was not the primary man in his girlfriend's life. Joel unconsciously worried that his father would still be jealous of any success that he had with a woman. The fantasy and the play-acting with his girlfriend were a way of saying to his father that some man other than Joel was the successful lover.

This also served to reassure his mother that he was still available to provide her with the companionship he thought she needed, by showing her that he was not the main source of pleasure to his girlfriend.

When we were able to clarify the meaning of the mind-sets that stimulated these fantasies, they began to gradually diminish. Over time, Joel's sex life with his girlfriend became more pleasurable.

Aloofness versus Responsiveness

In another story of double trouble, Dianne, a consultant, had a rejecting mother. As a child, Dianne learned to inhibit her need for affection, comfort, and reassurance. Her interest in being close to her mother caused her mother to feel burdened, leading her to distance herself from her daughter. In response to the rejection from her mother, Dianne became independent and emotionally aloof.

Dianne's father, on the other hand, needed too much closeness and affection from her. When she felt uncomfortable about being responsive, affectionate, and close to her father (because of her experience with her mother), he would act hurt and rejected by her.

This caused Dianne great distress and made it difficult for her to relate to men in general. She preferred men who were responsive to her, to compensate for her mother's coldness toward her. However, she had difficulty reciprocating their affection, fearing that she would be rejected by them.

When Dianne was responsive and emotional, her mother disapproved and her father was happy. When she was emotionally aloof, her mother approved and her father was unhappy. Thus, aloofness and emotional responsiveness were in conflict for Dianne.

Independence versus Neediness

A married business executive named Roberta came to me for therapy just after her father's death. What troubled her was the awareness that although she complained about her husband, job, and weight, she felt that these dissatisfactions weren't warranted. Her complaints and the depression that developed during the period of her father's terminal illness were even more pronounced after his death. At first I thought that Roberta's problems stemmed from the loss of her father, but that wasn't the case.

As she talked, I became aware that she was feeling sorry for her lonely mother. As we explored this theme, she began to realize that she was contrasting her successful life with that of her mother, who was unhappy, had nothing to do, was overeating, and was bouncing back and forth between her four children in order to feel involved with something.

Roberta described how difficult it was for her mother to relate to people who were independent and fulfilled in life, which resulted in her gravitating towards involvement with her two needy adult sons. In that way, her mother acquired meaning by "being a mommy."

Roberta, however, didn't need her mother, but she felt guilty about it. "I don't need her. My life is not a mess." To relieve her guilt feelings toward her mother, she felt obligated to develop complaints about her job, weight, and husband, all to make her mother feel more needed. These problems also served to relieve her guilt over feeling sorry for her mother.

Roberta's father expected her and her younger sister to be like him: punctual, responsible, and strong. As a result, Roberta grew up feeling she could handle any problem that was presented to her. Her mother, on the other hand, was weak and easily dominated by Roberta's father. He was contemptuous of his wife's weakness, which reinforced for Roberta the importance of being capable and resilient. Therefore, she was caught between the different requirements of each parent. Again, a problem of double trouble.

The independent mind-set Roberta had acquired from her father caused her to feel anxious if instead she acted weak and needy so that her mother could play a mothering role. Therefore, by accommodating to her mother's needs (by being weak and needing her help), she would strongly disappoint her father. But by effectively managing her life (which would make her father happy), Roberta deprived her mother of having a maternal role in her life.

When Roberta's father died, she felt even sorrier for her mother. She felt required to have problems so that her mother could continue mothering her in order to have meaning in her life. Roberta remained conflicted, because loyalty to her deceased father demanded that she be a strong, capable, and problem-solving woman.

Until her father's death, Roberta was able to maintain a psychological equilibrium because her mother wasn't lonely or obviously unhappy. Therefore, she didn't feel too guilty towards her mother and could more comfortably be successful in her own life. After her father died, Roberta began to unconsciously worry about her mother's loneliness and unhappiness.

Extracting what we can for our survival is crucial to our development. The parent who is most able to nurture us (the survival figure) is the one towards whom we develop the strongest attachment, even if it leads to conflicts of loyalty between our parents.

Joel developed his strongest attachment to his mother, who admired and supported him, even though making her happy made his insecure father feel threatened and jealous. Pleasing his father would have required him to continue to suppress his abilities at the price of disappointing his mother. Joel wasn't about to spoil his relationship with his mother, who was his survival figure. He navigated the troubled waters with difficulty because both success and failure caused him to feel guilty.

Another example of double trouble occurs when one child, in doing better than his or her sibling, pleases one parent but disappoints the other. The second parent wants the weaker or less successful one to do better and tragically assumes that discouraging the stronger one will accomplish that goal. Unfortunately, this attempt can't create a level playing field. The more successful child will resent both the parent and the sibling because of having to inhibit his or her goals, and will worry about disappointing the other parent by holding back. The weaker child will feel guilt about being the cause of the stronger sibling's resentment.

Look at the accompanying chart, Examples of Double Trouble. Do any of the patterns described reflect your situation?

In this book so far we have seen how mismatches can ruin your life, how you create moral commandments that interfere with your goals, how your thoughts can plague you, how adapting to your parents' and siblings' flaws can harm you, and how double trouble can further complicate your problems. Why, with many negative experiences and even with your conscious awareness of your problems, does your will to change often fail you? Why does the best advice from many self-help books fall short?

The knowledge you need to overcome your problems will be provided in the next two chapters.

EXAMPLES OF DOUBLE TROUBLE

Parent or Sibling A	Parent or Sibling B
Needs you to succeed to feel good. Lives through your accomplishments (looks, sports, grades, popularity).	Is competitive with you and is threatened by your success.
Is depressed and needy. You are overly attentive and worried about him or her.	Feels left out or rejected by your attention to the other parent.
Is rejecting toward you when you try to be close to him or her, causing you to become distant and self-contained.	Enjoys closeness and feels hurt by your aloof and distant attitude.
Wants you to be independent and strong.	Is possessive and upset by your independence from them. Wants to be able to baby you.
Prefers boys over girls. If you are a boy, you make this parent happy but displease the other.	Prefers girls over boys. If you are a boy, you will disappoint this parent.
Can't stand weakness or failure.	Can't stand strength.
Is emotionally explosive or labile. Drugs or alcohol may be involved. You become vigilant and worried about them.	Feels burdened by your vigilance and worry towards the other parent or towards him- or herself.
Is a failure, causing you to feel sorry for him or her. You fear doing well in life.	Lives through your accomplishments. Needs for you to be successful.

CHAPTER NINE

Why Is Willpower Not Enough?

YOU ARE HIGHLY MOTIVATED TO change, and yet you still can't stop behaving in ways you hate. You understand that mind-sets are created within your unconscious mind and remain hidden from view because of the ghosts of pain. Furthermore, you know that guilt contributes to and reinforces your mind-sets. You've begun to see how behavior in your family may have been responsible, but you know there is more. Beneath your conscious understanding lies another level of information and motivation. It's what makes your will to change completely ineffectual. What is it?

In many areas of life, you probably have excellent problem-solving skills. You know what effect your behavior will have on your life. For example, you know that if you do your job well, it will probably lead to an increase in salary or a promotion. You also know that studying hard for your exams will probably lead to good grades, and that being unfocused will lead to poor grades. It's obvious that if you are considerate of people, you will usually be well liked, and if you are rude you will be disliked. You know that if you are careful about saving and investing your money, it will probably lead to a prosperous retirement.

If you can figure out what will work to achieve your goals in these areas, why are your problems in other areas so resistant? What is still hidden from your understanding?

Remember the ghosts of pain that help to keep your mind-sets hidden? As we discussed in Chapter Four, you can't easily solve a problem if you don't understand its source. That's why it's so important to get rid of your mind-set ghosts. As you'll recall, they are empowered by guilt and pain. But once you expose them and you begin to see the behavior of other family members that contributed to your problems, you'll run smack into another reason to feel guilt. Unless you understand it you'll be unable to change.

Betrayal: A Reason to Feel Guilt

To clarify, let's explore the major reasons why you are blind when looking into relationships in your past.

YOU HAVE BETRAYED YOURSELF

More guilt? You bet! When you get a good look at the mind-set ghosts of pain you'll begin to feel remorse toward yourself. You'll recognize that you betrayed yourself.

You will feel the pain of knowing that you undermined your own present success (the ghost of present pain). You will be reminded of the original painful experiences with parents and siblings for which you wrongly took responsibility (the ghost of past pain).

You will become aware that because you falsely blamed yourself for parent's flaws, you do not feel deserving enough to pursue what is good for you (the ghost of future pain).

All of these examples of irrational self-blame can be a devastating betrayal of your life and ambition.

YOU WILL BETRAY OTHERS

We often view our parents more favorably than is justified by our experience with them. Why is that? You don't want to remember and reexperience the pain and sadness associated with the memories of having been hurt by your parents. You don't want to reexperience the blame you felt for hurting them. Consequently, you view them in a more favorable light than is warranted.

On the other hand, to correctly assign blame means that you may feel guilty about unmasking your parents' and siblings' faults and vulnerabilities. Especially if your parents or siblings are very hurt by criticism and therefore vulnerable to feeling exposed, you will feel guilty remembering their faults. Shedding the light of truth exposes your family members to feelings of humiliation and shame for which you feel responsible.

YOU HATE YOURSELF

Betrayal makes you damned if you do and damned if you don't. Have you ever noticed how angry it makes you feel when you notice that you have taken on the very qualities of your parents and siblings that you hated? As you see yourself mimicking something your parent did, why is the natural inclination to shrug it off or deny it rather than focus on it?

You'd have to expose yourself to self-criticism for not being free of a behavior you hate. It would be painful to think that you were motivated to mimic a parent or sibling to prevent them from feeling jealous of you. (You keep yourself from being better off if you are just like your parent or sibling.) In other words, you are still protecting them.

Your parents falsely blamed you for their faults. When they say things like "I hope your children do to you what you've done to me," your sense of guilt toward them makes you feel that you ought to be paid back (punished). You achieve this by mimicking them and then suffering in the same way from your children's behavior.

As an example, if your parent acted provoked and hurt when you demonstrated your intelligence, you would feel guilty for hurting them. To pay yourself back, you might mimic him or her and become threatened by your children when they showed their smarts.

These are some of the motivations that keep you blind to the truth.

YOU DON'T SEE THE TRUTH

You may know that your childhood was terrible, but you usually can't figure out how it specifically caused you to suffer in your adult life, because of the reasons just discussed. Let's examine this idea.

Over the years, many clients have come to my office with a history of an alcoholic parent or parents. Although they knew their childhood was difficult, what is of interest is how hard it was for each person to understand how he or she was actually affected by it.

For example, you may easily remember your mother or father's alcoholism but not see how it caused you to develop a specific limitation or behavior you hate. Although you may have had to regularly save your parent from an alcoholic stupor, you might not see how that caused you to become a rescuer of others. You might not see that feeling overly responsible for others at the expense of your own interests grew out of this same situation. You may be unaware that your inability to speak up or confront what you dislike developed from worry that your intoxicated parent would fly into a rage or become violent if you complained or challenged him or her.

Remember Rose the lawyer in Chapter Seven? She experienced great anxiety when she had to confront or disagree with anyone because this situation was associated with her childhood memories of her alcoholic father, who exploded into violent rages when confronted.

Those of you who are struggling with your own drinking problem might make the connection between your alcoholism and your parent's, but not understand what in your psychology prevents you from stopping drinking. For instance, if you are unaware that you blamed yourself for a parent's drinking, you will feel you deserve no better for yourself. You will become like your parent. As a result of your feelings of guilt, you'll be unable to free yourself of behavior you hate.

Any behavior you hate may be hidden due to your fear of betraying yourself or others. You may remember hating your father for his meanness, but because you blamed yourself for it, you may not be able to connect it with a specific problem such as being mean yourself.

You may be aware of your father's depression, but because you felt sorry for him, or blamed yourself for it, you may not realize how it caused you to feel depressed, or undeserving of having fun with your friends.

You may remember having an obese family member but not be clear about why you have difficulty controlling your weight. Did you feel sorry for him or her? Did you blame yourself for his or her eating problem? You may remember that one of your parents or siblings was self-centered, demanding continual admiration. Have you associated your problem with losing weight to your fear of being attractive and causing him or her to feel intense jealousy of you?

Is your obesity the result of rebelling against the pressure of a parent who needed you to be thin, beautiful, and perfect? Is your overeating a result of rebelling against a parent who withheld food from you to punish you?

You could easily remember your father's struggle to be successful in business but not connect it with your own pattern of continually losing money in the stock market.

You might remember how your parents worried about the poor performance of your brother or sister but not see that this caused you to do poorly in school or poorly at work later on.

You may remember being criticized all the time, but not realize that it is causing you to be disliked because you are critical of others.

You also may have no awareness of having been mistreated in your childhood but notice that you are having difficulties in your adult life. In fact, your difficulties may be related to having been given preferential treatment by your parent. Isn't it ironic that positive reinforcement can lead to a negative outcome? If, for whatever reason, you feel responsible for a sibling being mistreated by your parents, to recall his or her suffering could arouse strong feelings of self-blame.

Let me remind you of Fred, whose athletic and academic success was strongly admired by his father. But his younger brother was frequently beaten by their father for always getting into trouble and for doing poorly in school. Fred's father would yell at his brother, "Why can't you be like Fred?"

Fred felt responsible for outshining his brother and causing him to look bad in the eyes of their father. He irrationally blamed himself for the mistreatment his brother received. As a result, he began to limit his athletic and academic achievements.

Incidentally, Fred also worried that his father would be disappointed if he didn't perform well (double trouble), but that fear was not as powerful as his irrational self-blame for his brother's difficulties.

If Your Past Is Buried, Why Dig It Up?

First, not having the specific knowledge of the ways in which your parents adversely affected your development interferes with your ability to change your current behavior, because you may still be unconsciously blaming yourself for your parents' treatment of you instead of seeing how your parents caused your problems. So you must exhume your past to find out if you are still accepting blame for what was not your fault. Remember, if you think you are to blame, this sets you up as a criminal who doesn't deserve to have things go his or her way. The outcome will be that you will not believe that you deserve to feel good by freeing yourself from your problems.

Second, if you don't have the specific knowledge of how you were affected by your parents or siblings, you will not have adequate knowledge of cause and effect, and therefore will be unable to consciously address the problem. If, for example, you don't recognize that you are mistreating your child in the way your parent mistreated you, it will be difficult for you to face the problem and change how you are treating your child.

When You Feel Like a Sinner: How Guilt Interferes with Changing Your Life

As long as you believe that certain of your actions were responsible for hurting your parents, you will also believe that similar behavior will hurt others. Therefore, when others in your life such as friends, lovers, co-workers, and employers behave in ways similar to your parents, you will again respond in the same self-destructive ways. Furthermore, if you irrationally believe that you have hurt your parents and others, you will feel you deserve to suffer for it. Therefore, you will have to suffer, and as a result, you will continue to hold yourself back.

Remember, when you feel like a sinner, your guilt feelings will influence you to act self-destructively to punish yourself for your sins. As a sinner, you also may feel obligated to atone for your sins by rescuing others, even if it is at your own expense.

For example, if, like Fred, you believe that your success in school harms your siblings or parents, you may develop strong guilt feelings in relation to them and, as a result, get poor grades. These guilt feelings automatically become activated in other places and times when you again attempt to perform successfully, because (1) you irrationally believe that either your parents or siblings or someone new will be hurt by your successes, or (2) you still have so much guilt from feeling you hurt your parents or siblings in the past that you don't feel you deserve to ever be successful.

In another case, if you felt your father was unhappy and lacked self-esteem, and you associated this with your having been admired, you might feel obligated to cheer him up, help him with his problems, give him credit for any accomplishments, and downplay your own.

A WORRISOME DREAM

John, a thirty-nine-year-old man, fell madly in love with a woman he had been dating for two months and asked her to marry him. His close friend Charlie was also a single man with whom John partied. Charlie questioned John's decision to become committed to marriage so soon after meeting his fiancée and asked him if he was sure he had made the right decision. In addition, Charlie expressed a sense of nostalgia for the fun times they shared going out together to meet single women.

The night following this talk with his friend, John became withdrawn from his fiancée, which led to a big argument with her. When he saw me the next day, he described a dream he had had that night in which he was in bed with Charlie, who was playing with John's genitals.

John told me that he did not become aroused by his friend's actions and that he felt uncomfortable telling me about this dream. When I asked him what his thoughts were about it, he immediately said that it was interesting to him that Charlie had replaced his fiancée in bed. He also expressed relief that he had not been aroused by his friend's sexual overtures because of the homosexual aspect of the dream.

I suggested to John that he was experiencing guilt toward Charlie, who was feeling displaced and hurt by John's intense involvement with his fiancée. As a result, to relieve his guilt, he tried in his dream to comfort and appease his friend by becoming distant from his fiancée and instead becoming intimate with him. The lack of arousal showed that he was truly interested in his fiancée. John felt relieved by this interpretation and immediately resumed the romantic closeness he had previously felt with his fiancée.

What factors could have predisposed this outcome? The main factor in John's history was the effect on him of his brother's severe mental illness. The symptoms of his brother's illness showed up during his childhood as serious behavior problems in school, and progressed during adolescence and adulthood to include many hospitalizations. Because of the tremendous contrast between their lives and the admiration John received from his parents compared with their distress over his brother, John felt sorry for his brother and became very sensitive to anyone who was suffering.

Therefore, when John succeeded in meeting the woman of his dreams before Charlie did, it made him guilty about feeling better off than his friend. His current life situation had been impacted by his lifelong angst about his brother. John always had difficulty feeling better off than other people in his life. In this instance he used a dream to atone for his guilt towards Charlie.

CRIME AND PUNISHMENT:
WHY BE A VICTIM IF IT'S NO FUN?

Imagine that you have been arrested, convicted, and punished for someone else's crime. If you are trapped in behavior you hate, that's really what has happened. I call it psychological jail.

The Arrest   Like any imprisonment, it begins with an accusation. But in this case, you make it against yourself or allow someone else to make it and never speak in your own defense. Your natural urges and inclinations are brought under arrest.

Your Confession   During your early years, the accusation is repeatedly tested. Because you wrongly interpret the causes of other people's actions, you make internal confessions of guilt.

The Conviction   These internal confessions eventually lead to a mountain of emotional evidence against you. You become convinced that you are guilty as charged. You have done something wrong and deserve to be punished.

Sentencing   You are sentenced to atone for your crime for the rest of your life through the restriction of your freedom to pursue your own goals (see again the chart How to Discover the Cause of Your Problems, pages 69–71). Furthermore, you may not discuss the case or your guilt will increase. Any attempt to escape your prison will result in pain.

This is psychological jail. The key that locks the door is self-blame.

Psychological Jail and False Imprisonment

People with a conscience who feel they have done something wrong also feel they should be punished. The psychological equivalent of being punished is to not have the freedom to enjoy your life. You will therefore suffer and hate yourself for it.

Conversely, if you were in jail as a result of having been falsely accused of a crime, you would know that you shouldn't be there because you have done nothing wrong. The psychological equivalent of this is to be free from a false sense of guilt, and the resulting self-imposed restrictions. In other words, you'd feel perfectly justified to pursue your life goals.

You need to free yourself from irrational self-blame—your own false self-accusations of being responsible for hurting your parents or siblings—when in fact you were not at fault.

If you think you caused your mother's unhappiness, you will feel guilty and undeserving of feeling happy yourself. However, if you conclude that her unhappiness was unrelated to her relationship with you, you will feel fine about being happy. If you realize that your father's bad temper existed prior to your birth and wasn't connected to you, you won't feel you have to be punished for it. Therefore, you can free yourself from behavior you hate.

THE GOOTNICK TIME MACHINE

Remember, if you meet someone at a party who is a jerk, you don't assume responsibility for his or her behavior. You know it existed before you met and will continue after you leave. It isn't your fault.

Imagine what it would be like if you could enter my special time machine that would allow you to be reborn tomorrow, but with all the knowledge you've acquired about people during your whole adult life. Wouldn't your life have turned out differently? Of course it would. The reason is that you would be as unaffected by the flaws of your parents and siblings as you would when meeting someone at a party who is a jerk. You would know that those flaws existed before you were born and that they therefore had nothing to do with you.

Recall the example of the primitive tribe. The tribe avoids any behavior they think might cause a natural disaster because they feel irrationally responsible for offending the gods. Therefore, like children who irrationally blame themselves, they restrict their freedom to pursue their life goals. If instead they had a scientific explanation for the earthquake (knowledge of cause and effect), and as a result believed that the disaster had nothing to do with them, they would not feel guilty, would not have to atone for anything, and would feel free to go about their business as usual.

Remember imagining that you were an employee at a job you knew nothing about? Because you were unable to make the proper connections between cause and effect, you assumed it was your fault when the boss was angry. If instead you had all the information, such as the boss's true nature and what the job required of you, you could make the correct judgment about the reason for your boss's anger. Then you wouldn't have to irrationally blame yourself.

When you are a child and you feel you have done something wrong, you feel you deserve to be punished. Punishment and atonement cause you to restrict your freedom to pursue your goals. This is psychological jail, where you will be miserable without knowing why.

Just look at the outcome of some of these life sentences:

If you feel you caused your mother to complain and feel un-happy all the time, you might try to reduce your guilt towards her by also having complaints all the time. That would be your punishment for feeling that you made her unhappy. In this instance, all you would be aware of is how you hate yourself for being so unhappy. Now you will feel like a victim, without knowing the cause.

This self-inflicted punishment is payment for hurting your mother. You caused her to complain, so you deserve the same. In spite of hating her complaining and vowing to never act like that when you grew up, you may be shocked to find you have become just like her. If you feel the need to atone, you could try to do whatever you think would help your mother stop com-plaining and be happy, even at your own expense.

If you are a woman whose mother was mistreated or beaten by your father, but you were spared, you might conclude that her mistreatment was related to you being more appealing to your father. Your sense of guilt towards your mother would be even more intense if her misfortune occurred at a time when you were going through a normal developmental phase of competition with her for your father's attention. You could easily develop a strong sense of guilt towards your mother if you irrationally connect wanting to be preferred by your father with his cruelty toward her.

On that basis, you would feel guilty and try to reduce your guilt by also making yourself a victim of mistreatment. For ex-ample, you could inflict self-punishment by choosing a partner who was violent towards you the way your father was towards your mother. That would relieve your guilt towards your mother. In other words, you would pay for your crime by being no bet-ter off than she is.

If you feel you made your father unhappy by not paying enough attention to him, you can relieve your sense of guilt by feeling that he, your mother, or others aren't paying enough attention to you. All you would be aware of is how unpleasant it is to feel rejected all the time. This is how you punish yourself for thinking you rejected your father. Alternatively, you could try to relieve your guilt through atonement by paying extra attention to your father or others, even if it means you neglect your own interests.

If you feel that your father is jealous of your relationship with your mother, you can feel less guilty through self-punishment by making yourself feel jealous of someone else. Again, you would feel like a victim. All you would be aware of is how you hate yourself for feeling so envious of others. If you feel the need to atone for making your father feel jealous and left out, you could make it up to him by leaving yourself out of the relationship with your mother or with women in general.

As a result of blaming yourself for your parents' or siblings' problems, you punish yourself by suffering like your parents or siblings did. The result of this is that you in fact become like them. The purpose of this is to relieve your guilt towards them by being like them, rather than better off than they are. After all, you feel you don't deserve any better, since you feel you caused their problems in the first place. This explains why in spite of hating certain qualities in your parents and vowing to never be like them, you may end up with those same qualities.

You can see how guilt feelings get in the way of freeing yourself from behavior you hate, because these guilt feelings require punishment, atonement, and identification with your parents' bad qualities in order for you to feel any relief.

Pathological Jealousy

Pathological jealousy was introduced by the prosecution in the O. J. Simpson trial as the motive for the murder. What is the meaning of this term, and how does this condition develop?

When you have done something wrong, you feel you deserve to be punished and that your punishment should fit the crime. For example, if you have an affair, you begin feeling disloyal to your spouse. To assuage your guilt, you may punish yourself by making yourself feel betrayed by your spouse. As a result, you will notice yourself continually finding fault with the person you betrayed in order to feel victimized and betrayed in return. The greater your sense of guilt, the more enraged by your spouse you will become.

A person who feels extremely envious of another person is often unknowingly very uncomfortable about feeling envied by that person. In other words, he or she feels guilty about being better off than the other person and relieves those guilt feelings by thinking that the other person is much better off than he or she.

External crimes such as stealing are dealt with by external legal systems. But what about crimes that are internal? Your own internal legal system will send you to psychological jail.

Let's look at some examples that illustrate this.

Sylvia was a client of mine who hated herself for not being able to feel close to women or feel happy with men. During her childhood, Sylvia's sister was terribly jealous of her for being their father's favorite. As a result, without being aware of it, Sylvia suffered greatly by making herself feel envious of her women friends to atone for causing her sister to be jealous of her. She was trying to overcome feeling guilty that her sister and sister substitutes envied her for having a great boyfriend and eventually a great husband. All she was aware of was that she was feeling envious of her women friends and that she hated feeling that way.

Sylvia's other complaint was that she periodically had terrible fights with her husband, with whom she was otherwise extremely happy. As therapy progressed, she realized that her motive for these fights was to keep other women from feeling envious of her happiness with her husband. In other words, she tried to make herself unhappy through fighting. She gradually learned that this stemmed from the effect that her sister's jealousy had on her. Learning this freed her from feeling responsible for her sister's jealousy.

Sylvia realized that it was not her intention to make her sister jealous of her. She was not to blame for the fact that their father favored her. Conversely, once Sylvia understood that her sister's jealousy was not her fault, she began to feel happier with her husband.

Sylvia's experience with her sister had made her sensitive to feeling envied by women any time that life went well for her. These feelings became provoked whenever one of her woman friends was unsuccessful with a man, or was having problems with a husband. Once she learned about her mind-set, she stopped provoking unjustified fights with her husband. In addition, she no longer felt obligated to make herself feel envious of her women friends in order to atone for her sister's jealousy of her. What followed was that her relationships with these women became much more steady, fulfilling, and fun.

Who Is the Victim?

June, a married lawyer, came to me for therapy. She was having an affair and yet felt betrayed by her husband. As a result, she continually found fault and complained about him. At one point, she became sufficiently angry toward him to slap him during an argument. Why did June feel so victimized by her husband?

She was unconsciously feeling very guilty that she was hurting him by having an affair (thus making him a victim). She attempted to relieve her guilt by complaining and continually feeling hurt by him (thus making herself the victim). In other words, if she could feel hurt by him, she did not have to feel so bad about hurting him. When feeling hurt by him became extremely intense, it made her feel violent towards him. The greater June's fury about being victimized by her husband, the less guilty she had to feel towards him for her affair.

BEATING THE VICTIM

Have you ever noticed how often you see headlines like "Woman Murdered by Jilted Boyfriend" and wondered what the motivation was for such a gruesome act? As the result of having an affair, a client of mine named Mark felt so guilty towards his girlfriend that he pushed her into having an affair with a friend of his. This was an act of atonement. When, in response to being pushed away by him, his girlfriend would no longer go out with Mark, he went into a violent rage and beat her up. Since he had rejected her by having an affair, clearly his behavior was not based on being rejected by her. Instead, he was reacting to powerful feelings of guilt caused by having hurt her (through the affair) and felt the need to be punished for it in a similar way.

What predisposed Mark to this violence? It was his experience with his needy and overinvolved mother. She acted hurt whenever she felt disappointed by him. Her behavior made him extremely sensitive to her need for him, and therefore caused him to be over solicitous of her feelings. If he ignored what she needed and instead focused on his own needs, he experienced strong guilt towards her.

To solve his guilt, Mark developed victimization feelings in reaction to his mother. For example, when he returned from being out with his friends, he would complain about how she had neglected to do something he had requested of her. This might be something insignificant like not cooking what he liked to eat. Mark was making himself feel neglected by his mother to relieve his guilt about neglecting her (being with his friends instead of her).

This is exactly what happened with Mark's girlfriend. He unconsciously felt that by having an affair he was rejecting her. By feeling enraged when she stopped dating him, he made himself feel rejected by her in order to relieve his guilt for hurting her.

From this example, you can see that violence toward a partner can often occur without any apparent provocation. Instead, it is the outcome of severe unconscious guilt feelings that result from hurting the other person and having to deny it. The stronger your sense of guilt towards your partner, the more violent your anger towards that person. The rage and violence reflect how hurt you are by your partner and serve to exonerate you from having hurt her or him. Many murders are the result of this dynamic.

There are other causes of violence towards a loved one:

1. If you feel extremely sensitive to rejection as a result of having been severely rejected in your childhood, you might overreact and become violent if you are rejected again.
2. If you have been physically brutalized by a parent, you might do the same to a loved one in order to help yourself forget the pain of having been the victim of brutality. Watching someone else suffer helps you to repress the memories of your own suffering.
3. If one of your parents brutalized the other, you might learn by example to repeat the same behavior towards your partner.

Following are other examples of making yourself feel like a victim to relieve your feelings of guilt.

TAKEN FOR A RIDE

A client of mine, a young professional named Tom, was engaged and thrilled with his fiancée. He was doing well in his career and making a good living, and because his fiancée was in graduate school, Tom was happily paying for almost all of their expenses. Eventually, he began to feel resentment about paying for his fiancée's expenses, even though he could afford it and he had initially been pleased to do so. He confided to me that he felt she was taking advantage of him financially. He realized that his feelings of resentment didn't make much sense, and he wondered what could be causing them.

It turned out that Tom's lawyer had been suggesting that he have his fiancée sign a prenuptial agreement, based on the fact that 50 percent of all marriages end in divorce. Tom resisted the idea because he felt that a prenuptial agreement implied that he wasn't truly committed to the marriage. However, he did finally admit that his lawyer's advice made some sense. He also realized that he was worried about taking advantage of and hurting his fiancée by considering a prenuptial agreement. To relieve his guilt, he had made himself feel taken advantage of financially. Once he understood this, Tom's resentment disappeared.

BLOWING HIS COOL

In another case, a client named Lloyd, a tough businessman, was unable to ask anyone to do anything for him in a calm way. Instead, he became very angry whenever he had to make a request. He behaved this way even with his employees, even though he was in authority and knew that they would readily agree to what he asked. Having to ask someone else to do something make Lloyd made feel put upon.

Ironically, his problem stemmed from the fact that he felt he was burdening or imposing on others when requesting something from them. On the surface Lloyd appeared angry, when in fact he was actually feeling guilt when making demands of others. Therefore, he punished himself by making himself feel the victim as payment for thinking he was victimizing others.

Survivor Guilt

It is a common experience for people to suffer when they have survived terrible disasters in which others suffered or died. This phenomenon, known as "survivor guilt," is found in soldiers who live to tell about their experiences and in Holocaust survivors who lived when others in their families perished. Survivor guilt is irrational when the survivors had nothing to do with the misfortune of those who suffered or died.

Nonetheless, in many instances, in spite of being happy to be alive, survivors feel unworthy of having survived. This irrational guilt is similar to the guilt children experience as the result of thinking they have hurt their parents. Many people have preexisting experiences from childhood that predispose them to unreasonably blame themselves when things go wrong (or, like Fred, feel bad when things go right!). These individuals are likely to experience great emotional disturbance when surviving tragedies that others succumbed to.

In the movie *Ordinary People,* the son who survived the boating accident that killed his brother suffered from survivor guilt, causing him to make a suicide attempt, even though he had tried to save his brother from drowning. The surviving son's sense of guilt was intensified by the agony his mother suffered over the loss of her favorite son. This caused him to be more susceptible to accepting unjustified blame. In order to relieve her sense of loss, his mother acted cold and unsympathetic towards her surviving son. He unconsciously accepted blame in order to accommodate to her and relieve her suffering.

A professional man named Steve came to me for therapy because of his depression following a severe heart attack, which caused significant damage to his heart. After undergoing successful bypass surgery, Steve was told that he would have to retire but that he would be able to be moderately active, play golf, go for walks, travel, and engage in sex with his wife.

Steve was relieved that he did not have to return to his very stressful career, and was also relieved that he did not have to be concerned about his finances because of adequate disability insurance. In spite of the opportunity to enjoy his life and family, however, he became depressed.

Years earlier, Steve's father had suffered a heart attack and had been unable to make a good adjustment to his changed circumstances. As a result of excessive anxiety, his father had become a "cardiac cripple" and in the process was totally unable to enjoy his remaining years. In spite of advice to do so, the father refused bypass surgery and instead lived every day in fear of dying.

Before his father died, on a few occasions he complained to his son of chest pain. Steve told him to call his doctor and have it checked out. But his father, in denial, assumed it was indigestion and did nothing. He died a short time after. Steve experienced an *irrational sense of blame* for his father's death, even though he had told his father to contact his doctor immediately.

Steve felt that he should have instead told his father that the chest pain was most likely caused by his heart disease. His sense of guilt interfered with Steve's ability to take advantage of the opportunity to enjoy the rest of his life. His father's inability to more successfully manage his life after the heart attack, in combination with Steve's irrational sense of responsibility, made it difficult for him to feel that he deserved to enjoy his own life.

The second cause of Steve's inability to enjoy his retirement was his relationships with his family members. He was the only one in his family who had become a professional, and his achievements were profoundly important to his parents' self-esteem. As a result, from childhood on he had been strongly motivated to achieve great things in life in order to fulfill his family's need for glory. Now that Steve was no longer able to perform in his career, he unconsciously worried that he was letting his family down. This made him feel that he didn't deserve to enjoy retirement.

Moving On

Coming up next is a chart called Checking Out Your Symptoms (pages 125–127). Take the time to locate the symptom that represents behavior you hate. See if your symptoms are in response to accommodating to, rebelling against, or mimicking your parents' and/or siblings' behavior. Then move on to the next chapter, which explains how some circumstances can make it easier for you to change.

Your Symptom or Problem	Your symptom is a result of trying to not hurt or threaten your parent or sibling.	Your symptom is a rebellion or protest against what they expect of you.	You mimic your parent or sibling. You don't feel you deserve to be better off than they.
You overeat and are overweight.	1. They are unattractive, insecure about their looks and weight, and jealous of those who are attractive. Thus they are competitive with you. 2. They need you to eat in order to feel fulfilled.	1. Your parent (or sib) is overly worried about your eating habits or choices of food. They need you to be thin. 2. They may have withheld desserts as punishment.	Your parent (or sib) overeats and is overweight.
You are a failure in business, career, and at making money. You may be a gambler.	They are insecure about money and are jealous of wealthy and successful people. They brag about their skill with money.	Your parent (or sib) strongly needs you to be successful and wealthy in order to feel fulfilled in life.	Your parent (or sib) has failed in their career, business, or at making money. They may have been gamblers.
You feel insecure and inadequate without cause.	Your parent (or sib) has excessive pride and needs to show off and brag in order to feel worthwhile.	Your parent (or sib) needs you to be strong and independent. You protest by being insecure.	Your parent (or sib) is insecure and inadequate.
You have to show off and be the center of attention.	Your parent (or sib) feels inadequate and lives through your achievements to feel self-esteem.	Your parent (or sib) prefers that you be shy and retiring. He or she detests people who show off.	Your parent (or sib) is self-centered and has to show off.

CHECKING OUT YOUR SYMPTOMS, Continued

Your Symptom or Problem	Your symptom is a result of trying to not hurt or threaten your parent or sibling.	Your symptom is a rebellion or protest against what they expect of you.	You mimic your parent or sibling. You don't feel you deserve to be better off than they.
You suffer and complain all the time.	They resent your sense of well-being and need to feel superior.	Your parent (or sib) expects you to keep your pain and problems to yourself.	Your parent (or sib) complained, suffered, and acted like a victim.
You are compliant and do what you are told. You are a yes-man. You strictly follow the rules.	Your parent (or sib) is authoritarian and controlling, and possibly rigid.	Your parent (or sib) wants you to be a rebel or a nonconformist, or they are rebellious nonconformists.	Your parent (or sib) does what he or she is told, and is a yes-man.
You are shy and avoid the limelight.	Your parent (or sib) needs to be the center of attention.	Your parent (or sib) wants you to perform and be center stage.	Your parent (or sib) is shy and avoids the limelight.
You avoid closeness with others.	1. Your parent (or sib) is rejecting towards you and/or burdened by closeness. 2. The parent of the same sex competes with you for the other parent.	Your parent (or sib) is possessive and wants you to only be close to them.	Your parent (or sib) avoids closeness with others.
You are dependent and needy.	Your parent needs to mother or baby you.	Your parent (or sib) is rejecting. Your parent (or sib) wants you to keep your distance from him or her.	Your parent (or sib) is dependent and needy.

You have to be right.	through your intellectual achievements.	or usually wrong.	about life.
You compulsively yell.	They need to feel superior by always being in control.	1. They didn't pay attention to you. 2. They couldn't tolerate any expression of emotion.	They yelled all the time.
You steal or cheat.	They need to feel morally superior and righteous.	They deprived you, cheated you, used you.	They are dishonest and cheat and steal.
You are excessively mistrustful of others.	They expect you to trust and depend only on them.	They are naive and overly trusting. They are easily taken advantage of.	They are mistrustful or paranoid.
You have many affairs but run the other way when the other person falls in love with you.	1. The parent of the same sex competes with you for the other parent. 2. Your parent (or sib) was very rejecting 3. Your parent (or sib) lives vicariously through your sexual conquests.	1. Your parent (or sib) was too involved with you, making you feel smothered or trapped. 2. They were overly moralistic about sex.	Your parent (or sib) had many affairs and was uncomfortable showing affection to his or her spouse.
You choose partners who reject you.	A parent (or sib) is jealous, hurt, and rejected by your relationship with the other parent or other people.	Your parent (or sib) needs you to have ideal, blissful relationships with others.	Your parent, usually of the same sex, is rejected by the other parent.
You are self-reliant and avoid showing your feelings.	Your parent (or sib) is rejecting and lacks sympathy and empathy for you.	Your parent (or sib) is overly depressed and needy of sympathy and caring.	Your parent (or sib) is indifferent to the suffering or needs of others.

Your Symptom or Problem	Your symptom is a result of trying to not hurt or threaten your parent or sibling.	Your symptom is a rebellion or protest against what they expect of you.	You mimic your parent or sibling. You don't feel you deserve to be better off than they.
You are a rescuer and over-sensitive to people in need.	Your parent (or sib) is needy, unhappy, or mistreated. Requires attention from you.	Your parent (or sib) is indifferent to suffering.	Your parent (or sib) is a rescuer and do-gooder.
You please and accommodate others. You give in too easily.	Your parent (or sib) is very demanding and authoritarian, or needy and guilt-provoking.	Your parent (or sib) wants you to be stubborn and uncooperative.	Your parent (or sib) pleases and accommodates others.
You are perfectionistic and are never satisfied with your accomplishments.	Your parent (or sib) lives through your accomplishments, but is never satisfied with them.	Your parent (or sib) wants you to fail or makes fun of you when you make mistakes, is competitive with you.	Your parent (or sib) has to be perfect.
You are extremely vigilant, worried, and insecure.	Your parent (or sib) uses drugs, alcohol, or is mentally unstable and unpredictable.	Your parent (or sib) is in denial whenever a crisis occurs.	Your parent (or sib) is anxious, vigilant, or worried.
You are a liar.	Your parent (or sib) needs to look good and feel good. He or she is vulnerable to the truth.	1. Your parent (or sib) is moralistic or rigid about telling the truth. 2. Your parent (or sib) is critical and finds fault with you.	Your parent (or sib) never tells the truth.

CHAPTER TEN

Circum-stances That Allow You to Change

ALTHOUGH IT IS NOT EASY, change is possible. In examining some of the reasons why change is so difficult, we learned that one obstacle to change is the difficulty of accurately remembering your past. If you did recall events from the past clearly, you would then be reminded of the painful experiences with your parents or siblings that led to holding yourself back. That is one reason why you may deny much of what you see in your parents and give them better grades than they deserve. As we discussed, as a child you tended to blame yourself for the problems your parents and siblings have. As a result, you want to block out the past and not remember feeling like a criminal who ruined things for others. If you can view your parents in a better light, you won't feel as guilty for thinking you caused their problems. On the other hand, there are some people who try to deny their false sense of blame by exaggerating the faults of their parents. *If you can't remember your past and see the true causes of your problems, it is difficult to change them, even by an act of will.*

Still, it is possible to change the behavior you hate. In order to do so, you need to feel protected from situations that you feel are dangerous, and from the unpleasant emotions and memories that may arise when you examine the causes of your behavior. Here are some some examples of conditions in everyday life that can help you to change your behavior.

What do the following circumstances have in common? (1) You have a close call on a highway and then later experience a rush of anxiety. (2) You watch a sporting event, and after your team wins, you notice yourself feeling sad.

Why should you begin to feel anxious when you are sitting safely on the side of the road, instead of while you are behind the wheel at the time of the close call? Similarly, why wouldn't you feel elation instead of sadness when the team you were rooting for achieves victory?

Both of these situations make it safe for you to experience dangerous emotions that you are holding back. If you allowed yourself to experience fear while you were driving, you would add to the danger of the situation. At the time of the close call you need to be calm and controlled in order to save your life. Therefore, only when you are safely parked at the side of the road can you allow yourself to experience the feelings that were previously too dangerous to feel.

Similarly, when you are watching a sporting event, you might not be aware that you are holding back sadness or other unpleasant emotions associated with your past failures. *Watching others succeed allows you to identify with their success.* You think to yourself that you can have the same success. This might be sufficiently reassuring to allow you to experience the repressed sadness associated with your lifelong difficulties with competition and success. Therefore, you become paradoxically sad when your team wins.

We often distance ourselves from painful experience and feelings until we feel safe. Because these original feelings were so painful, they are kept out of our awareness until someone else's success makes it safer for us to feel our own repressed sadness.

The principle common to both of these examples is that when circumstances and relationships allow us to feel protected from feelings or actions that are dangerous, we can allow ourselves to experience them, or to even examine them. Let's look at some real-life situations that are based on this principle.

Odd Couples

People choose partners for many different reasons. In many cases, a person will choose a partner with opposite personality traits, which can easily lead to discord. How might that help someone to change his or her behavior? You might assume that there would be many conflicts associated with a couple having opposite qualities. How would a timid, weak, unassertive person become stronger if his or her partner is domineering? Wouldn't a shy person be more inhibited with a very outgoing person? In the play *The Odd Couple,* the compulsive man is continually exasperated by his scattered and disorganized roommate. So what motivated him to select such a person for a roommate? Have you ever seen a totally mismatched couple and thought, "What do they see in each other?" or "How do they get along?"

Although such pairings might seem like mismatches, one of the reasons people choose certain partners is to compensate for shortcomings in themselves. We are often missing certain qualities because we inhibited them in relation to our parents or siblings or because our parents didn't have those qualities.

For example, you might have been inhibited from being independent because of a possessive parent. You might have accommodated to a domineering family member by limiting thinking for yourself. If your parents were rigid and you imitated them, you would probably have kept yourself from being flexible in your outlook. Or you could have restricted your ambition because you felt sorry for someone in your family who was unfortunate or failing in life.

When we are missing certain abilities or traits, we want to acquire them. We can do this by learning from another person how to act more effectively. If you are a disorganized person, watching your compulsive partner be more organized helps you learn how to be that way too. If you are the compulsive one, struggling with wanting to be more free and more spontaneous, you may overcome some of your inhibitions by watching your partner act more freely. Similarly, if you are shy, you can become more social as a result of imitating and learning from an outgoing partner.

In all of these examples, the partner who has the desired traits demonstrates to you how to handle situations that you

have difficulty with. The partner with the admired traits is probably not motivated by the same destructive mind-set that holds
you back. This is reassuring, because if you are the person with
the weakness or the behavior you hate, it demonstrates that you
can learn to have different beliefs about life and therefore different attitudes and behavior.

Getting Support for Your Goals

If you think back on your own childhood experiences, you
can probably recall a special connection with a teacher, an aunt
or uncle, a friend's parent, a coach, or another adult who
had a positive impact on you. This occurred for two important
reasons:

First, that person had behavior and attitudes that you
wanted for yourself but had or had not developed yet. Second,
they were providing substitute experiences for you that you were
deprived of in your family. One is modeling what you need and
the other is replacing what you didn't get.

For example, your mentor or role model might have encouraged you to do well in school or sports when your parents
were indifferent or threatened by your success. Your mentor/role
model may have shown you compassion and caring when you
were having problems or feeling troubled, something your parents may not have been able to do for you. This special person
might have accepted you for who you were, as opposed to your
parents, who expected you to perform in a particular way, as a
condition of appreciating you.

If your parents were burdened by or indifferent to your need
for guidance, you might have felt helped by a mentor who gave
you special advice when you were uncertain about what to do.
If as a result of feeling encouraged by such a person, you over-
came worries about being envied for your success, you could
feel less inhibited about competing. This kind of guidance would
have helped you because it compensated for specific deficiencies
in your parents.

Similar gains may take place as a result of participating in
sports and in support groups (which are teams of a sort). In

these activities we benefit from having experiences that were missing in our childhood, as well as from having role models to show us how to do what is difficult for us.

A young man who holds himself back because of the belief that he will hurt his sibling by doing well may feel less guilty and encouraged to do well as a result of belonging to a support group, team, or fraternity. The support of others may undermine the power of a destructive mind-set that others will be hurt by his success. The support he receives helps to relieve him of feeling responsible for his sibling's problems. *When we feel less irrational self-blame, we feel more justified to do well for ourselves.*

Also, when we notice people in our group who are not afraid to do well, they provide an example to us of what is possible. This shows us that there are people who are motivated in life by mind-sets different from our own. What a relief.

This kind of success can occur in weight-loss groups because mutual support diminishes the power of mind-sets to keep people overweight. If, for example, you are overweight and are worried about being better off than someone in your family who is also overweight, or if you are afraid of feeling envied for being good-looking, or you feel uncomfortable about being sexually attractive, or you are worried about gaining independence from a parent, or if you are heavy to protest against parents who needed you to be perfect (thin and beautiful), the support and acceptance you will receive from others in such a group will help to offset and to undermine the beliefs that contributed to your being overweight.

Although such support groups are often very useful, you will have even more success if you understand the mind-set that caused your problem in the first place. *With awareness comes the potential for getting rid of behavior you hate.* I will show you how to achieve this in the next few chapters.

We have discussed odd couples and the ways in which they can help each other. But what about relationships in which one partner mistreats or behaves badly towards the other? How could this be helpful? Even in these situations it is possible to learn to resist acting in ways you hate.

Fighting in Order to Make Love

Have you ever wondered why some couples fight as a precondition to making love? Why isn't their fighting followed by acting distant, carrying a grudge, or sulking, as it is for others? What advantage does this harsh method of interacting serve for them?

For some, fighting allows one or both partners to feel safe about the danger of closeness. What mind-sets might make it dangerous to feel close and make love? One is the fear that being too close may obligate you to excessively please your partner at your own expense. Another is the danger that if you love too strongly, you will be unable to protect yourself from being taken advantage of, or from rejection. A third is to relieve your hidden guilt about having a successful relationship. In other words, if you fight a lot, you can hide from yourself that you have a good relationship.

If you are struggling with damaging mind-sets like those just described, fighting can prove to you that you have the capacity to create distance, act assertively, be in control, and not be trapped. It can make you less afraid of being rejected or taken advantage of. If you are worried that your partner is weak and easily hurt, and you fear that as a result you have to act very cautious or protectively toward him or her, that person's ability to fight back will reassure you. Thus, choosing a partner who makes fighting possible creates an environment that enables you to overcome your fear of closeness. As a result it will be easier for you to achieve the intimacy that is associated with sex.

Petra was an attractive, divorced woman who came to me for help because of her problems with men. She usually attracted sensitive, caring, accommodating men, but was unable to fall in love with them. What perplexed her was her tendency to provoke fights with her partners. Soon after beginning therapy she became involved with a man named Don, who was very critical of her, causing them to fight all the time. It was with Don that Petra, paradoxically, developed an intense sexual involvement. It distressed her greatly that fighting or mistreatment was necessary for her to feel passion. What motivated this unpleasant dilemma?

When men adored Petra she experienced them as weak, dependent, and vulnerable. She was afraid that if she reciprocated their interest and enthusiasm, they would fall too much in love with her and become even more vulnerable to being hurt by her. Therefore, she restrained her emotions and interest in these men. Provoking fights was a way to learn if they could demonstrate strength and independence by fighting back. Petra misinterpreted Don's continual criticism of her to mean that he didn't need her and wouldn't become dependent on her. That reassured Petra that she didn't have to worry about hurting him. This enabled her to experience an intense, exciting sexual relationship with him.

Petra's story shows that the power of mind-sets can be overcome to some degree by situations and relationships that make your goals and actions seem less threatening.

Do you recall Mary from Chapter Two? Because she blamed herself for her father's disinterest in her mother, she provoked men to fight with her in order to not be better off than her mother.

Coping with a Disabled Sibling

A change in the life of a client named George made it possible for him to face his powerful feelings of survivor guilt. George had difficulty feeling happy and successful in life until his brother died. His brother had suffered from a severe physical handicap that prevented him from leading a full life. George was capable and talented but was burdened by a strong sense of survivor guilt towards his brother, feeling that it was unfair that he had so much in life compared with him.

His feelings of guilt interfered with George's freedom to feel happy. Therapy helped him to achieve moderate advances towards his goal of being happier by revealing his destructive mind-set that it wasn't right for him to be well off.

However, after most advances, George would experience some setbacks. He would complain a lot, feel pessimistic about his future, and deny that he had accomplished anything. He would get relief from his gloomy moods when I pointed out that his negative outlook was helping him to not feel so guilty towards his brother. Feeling this way was almost like talking directly to his brother, telling him to not feel so badly about his life since George too was miserable. Understanding this relieved George's guilt and helped him to feel happier.

After his brother died, George began to feel better more consistently. At first he felt embarrassed admitting that he was relieved that his brother was dead. After overcoming this embarrassment, however, George described how much easier it was to no longer have to observe his brother's terrible life and feel pity and sorrow for his brother.

What was most painful for George was not being able to do anything about his brother's suffering. Not being able to help his brother made it extremely difficult for George to overcome his survivor guilt. Now that his brother's ordeal was over, so was his. His brother was dead and George's survivor guilt was diminished, resulting in a significant behavioral change. It was now safer for George to be happy and successful.

Learning to Face Family Suffering

Dolores from time to time experienced terrible suffering, both with her husband and, later on, with her therapist. She grew up in an alcoholic family where both parents and a sister suffered emotional distress to an incredible degree. In addition, both of her parents made her responsible for rescuing them from their misery, drunkenness, and vicious fights.

Fortunately for Dolores, her husband and her therapist were not cold or insensitive to her. They were for the most part unprovoked by her distress, and did not require her to be responsible for their well-being. This helped her to not become overwhelmed and impaired when dealing with the responsibilities in her life. How did this seemingly cold behavior of her husband and therapist help her?

Dolores was struggling with this destructive mind-set from her childhood: "It is wrong to be in control of my life and to experience fulfillment while my family is suffering so badly. Since I feel that by paying attention to my life ignores their suffering, I am a terrible person who should suffer like them." By suffering in her adult life, Dolores unconsciously wanted to see if people close to her could tolerate the kind of suffering from her that as a child she found intolerable in her family.

Both Dolores's husband and therapist demonstrated to her that it was possible to be confronted with suffering, not be overwhelmed by it, and still manage your life effectively. Ultimately, they served as role models for her because they demonstrated that they were not operating with the same mind-set that she was. In other words, they weren't provoked the way she had been by the terrible suffering of someone close to them.

On the other hand, if a person's deep suffering were based on childhood experiences of rejection, insensitivity, and coldness, that person would require a spouse and therapist to be much more sensitive and supportive in response to his or her suffering. Without that support (replacing what was missing in his or her childhood), such a person's anxiety and suffering would intensify, not diminish, as it had in Dolores's situation.

Learning to Face an Overbearing, Arrogant Parent

Richard was a young attorney in his late twenties who hated himself for being unsuccessful with people in general and with women in particular. He managed to begin relationships with women, but almost always was rejected by them. What offended them was his pedantic, arrogant, self-righteous behavior, which they experienced as overbearing.

Paradoxically, Richard thought of himself as a considerate, caring person and was both surprised and hurt when he received such negative feedback. Leah was interested in him and tolerated his behavior because she found him interesting and stimulating. But he had very mixed feelings about her.

On the one hand, Richard felt contempt for her because he perceived her to be weak for not objecting to his behavior, which was similar to his father's. More importantly, he unconsciously appreciated her for tolerating his behavior, because she demonstrated that she could endure with him what he couldn't tolerate with his father. Leah had become a role model for Richard.

Richard had the mind-set "Father needs to feel superior and will feel threatened if people see me as a considerate, sensitive person. Therefore, I will be arrogant and overbearing like him to keep him from feeling threatened." Richard had been completely unaware that he was treating people in the same way his father had, and that therefore he could relate only to the few who could tolerate his behavior.

Richard's girlfriend demonstrated to him that it was possible to tolerate overbearing behavior. He was able to learn from his girlfriend's capacity to not be outraged by his arrogance. By learning from Leah how to not be outraged by arrogant behavior, Richard was able to more easily tolerate his father's arrogance. As a result, he was able to become less overbearing himself. Leah's ability to maintain her sensitivity towards Richard helped him to become more sensitive towards others.

Both this example and that of Dolores demonstrate the importance of choosing partners who serve as role models for learning how to face what is difficult for you.

The next chapter explains how to create personality profiles for your mother, father, siblings, and yourself, an important step in learning more about why you behave the way you do. Establishing these profiles will help you use the charts in this book more easily. That will make it easy to learn about the mind-sets, moral commandments, critical thoughts, and behaviors you hate, which you developed in relation to your family history.

The process of developing self-awareness may be analogous to trying to improve your looks as you go through life, without ever having had access to a mirror. Once you acquire one, you can determine whether it is your hair, complexion, skin, or teeth that need attending to, and then do something about it.

CHAPTER ELEVEN

Finding the Skeletons!

UP TO NOW WE HAVE USED EXAMples of other people to help you understand how hidden beliefs lead to self-destructive behavior. But you aren't reading this book just to learn about other people; you want to know about your own problem. You want to understand your parents, your siblings, and yourself. Now it is time to focus on you.

You may already know or have figured out the major flaws of your parents and siblings. If you are still unclear about these flaws and how they may have affected you, use the following personality profiles to uncover them.

Take your time to answer the following set of questions. Write the answers out so you can refer back to them if you need to. The object of creating personality profiles is to uncover things that are hidden. Doing so will help you to see the truth. Knowing the real underlying causes of your problems will empower you to act in your own behalf instead of being controlled by unknown forces. The following exercise can serve as a guide to discovering the causes of the behavior you hate.

You can answer these questions by yourself or together with your partner or friends. Completing personality profiles of your family and yourself with others can help to develop mutual understanding of each other's problems and their origins. Seeing how your family experiences shaped you and your partner or friends can promote mutual support and caring.

Personality Profiles

To discover the most damaging and problematic qualities of your parents and siblings, answer the following set of questions. We'll begin with your father. You can then reword the same exercise to create profiles of your mother, siblings, and other family members important to you during your childhood.

ASSESSING YOUR FATHER

1. What behavior did you hate the most in your father? How did he manifest it?
2. What situations in your family provoked that behavior, or made it worse?
3. What situations in your family made your father behave better?
4. What did you think was your role in those situations in which your father behaved badly?
5. When you wished that someone else could be your father, what qualities did that person have that were different from those of your father?
6. Who were the people outside your immediate family who made a large, positive difference in your life? What qualities did they have, and what did they offer you?

Once you've answered these questions about your father, complete a personality profile for your mother. Then do one for each sibling. Finally, include any other family members who were significant during your childhood. Now, complete the following personality profile for yourself.

ASSESSING YOURSELF

Ask yourself the following questions:

1. What behavior in yourself do you hate most?
2. If you could be anyone else, whom would you choose, and why?
3. Which situations provoke the behavior you hate in yourself?

4. Which situations make your behavior worse, and which situations make it better?
5. What kind of behavior did your parents or siblings display that you hated but that you in turn display to your children, partner, and others?
6. Write a letter to your parents and/or siblings explaining what you wish had been different in your relationship with them during your childhood.

When you have answered these questions, find your parents and/or siblings on the chart How to Discover the Cause of Your Problems (page 69), then find where you fit. Then find yourself on the chart Checking Out Your Symptoms (page 125). Hopefully, this will help you to understand how you developed the behavior you hate and to realize that it is a result of either accommodating to, rebelling against, or mimicking your parents and/or siblings. You may also discover that by acting like a family member, you do to others what he or she did to you.

Remember, you weren't the cause of your parents' and/or siblings' unhappiness! You were the victim of their problems! That means that you are not responsible for their flaws. You must appreciate this truth, because it will allow you to feel less guilty toward your family and more deserving of doing well for yourself. It will allow you to rid yourself of the behavior you hate.

SAMPLE ASSESSMENTS
The following assessments by one man illustrate how this process works.

Assessing Your Father

What behavior did you hate most in your father? How did he manifest it?   "The behavior I hated most in my father was his inability to feel confident and successful at anything he tried. He continually failed in his businesses and acted demoralized about his inability to make money. His morale and self-image were so diminished that he became overly preoccupied with his plight and was unable to adequately focus on the other people in his family. As a result he tended to withdraw to watch TV. He almost never complimented me or others. He smoked and over-ate, and he was unable to overcome either habit even when his health was bad. The way he dealt with his poor self-image was to try to make himself the center of attention or to insist that he was right. He was quick to see faults in others, but was defensive or in denial about his own."

What situations made his behavior worse?   "He had a difficult time making a living, and this sense of frustration worsened whenever he had business or financial pressures. He borrowed money from relatives and resented them and himself for it. This added to his low self-esteem, which caused him to overeat, lose his temper, and become withdrawn. He would often complain, 'Things are too much for me.' When he was in such a state of mind, he might break down and cry during an argument."

What situations made his behavior better?   "Paying attention to him made him feel more important. He felt especially good when he could be the center of attention, when people laughed at his jokes, or when they complimented him."

What was your role in those situations in which he acted badly?
"Whenever I was successful at something and got attention from the rest of my family, he became more dejected and withdrew from me. It was very difficult to get him to play sports with me or to show interest in my school activities."

When you wished someone else could be your father, what qualities did that person have that were different from your father's?
"I wished that my uncle could be my father because he exuded self-confidence, was effective with people, and was successful in his career. As a result, he was admired by everyone in the family. Life seemed easy for him in contrast with how burdened my father seemed. My uncle was knowledgeable about people, politics, and philosophy. I thought that if he could be my father instead I would feel happier about myself."

Who were the others in your life who made a difference to you?
"Teachers who appreciated my accomplishments and were en-

couraging to me inspired me to accomplish my goals. It seemed to make it easier for me to be successful in school, sports, and career when I had a mentor. I guess I was looking for a father substitute who was both self-confident and supportive of me."

Summary   You can see that this father was a failure in business, and was self-centered and competitive to compensate for feelings of inadequacy and insecurity. As a result, he felt threatened by his son's accomplishments and was unable to compliment or pay attention to him. As a result, his son assumed that his successes intensified his father's insecurity. When his son found mentors who served as positive father figures, he had an easier time pursuing his ambitions.

Assessing Your Mother

What behavior did you hate most in your mother?   "My mother seemed unhappy and disappointed with my father and made excuses for his inadequacies. She complained a lot and seemed to always need cheering up. So I spent a lot of time talking with her."

What made her behavior worse?   "She worried more when my father was withdrawn and got caught up in his worries about money. She seemed burdened by the need to make my father feel better. Even when things seemed all right she had some physical problem to complain about."

What made her behavior better?   "She seemed happier with me and with my relatives than with my father. She enjoyed my accomplishments, admired my ambition, and enjoyed talking to me. When I performed well in school and sports, or was complimented by neighbors, teachers, or relatives, she was happy. She also seemed to enjoy the time she spent with her brother or sister more than with my father."

What was your role in those situations in which she acted badly? "When I didn't pay enough attention to her, she became less happy."

When you wished someone else could be your mother, what qualities did that person have that were different from your mother's?   "I wished that one of my friend's mothers was my mother because she seemed happier, self-assured, and less needy of attention, and she didn't complain. A friend of the family was also like that. She was always glad to see me and didn't need to hear that I had accomplished something special in order to like me. She was upbeat and generally happy."

Summary   This mother seemed needy, complained a lot, and was unhappy with her husband. She focused on her son for satisfaction and was disappointed when he didn't pay enough attention to her. This made her son feel obligated to cheer her up and do things she could be proud of. Thus, he grew up to avoid anyone who complained and was needy and unhappy.

Assessing Your Sibling

What behavior in your sibling do you hate?   "My brother was much younger than I was, and my relationship with him was more that of a parent than a brother. What I disliked was having to take care of him because my parents worked. It wasn't that I disliked him but that I resented the burden of having to come home right after school to take care of him. There were many times that I hated him because he interfered with my spending time with my friends."

What made this behavior better, and what made it worse?   "When my parents were unavailable, I had to take time out of my life to do things with my brother like helping him with his homework, making sure he practiced the piano, and making his dinner. When my parents were available and took responsibility for him, that freed me to do more of the things I enjoyed."

What did you think was your role in those situations where your sibling behaved badly?   "He actually didn't behave badly. It was that I resented having to be a parent substitute for him. He always looked up to me and wanted to tag along."

Summary Responsibility for his brother made this man feel burdened and resentful. As a result, the mind-set he had developed, based on his relationship with his mother, was reinforced, and in adulthood he avoided anyone who was needy and dependent.

Assessing Yourself This sample assessment shows how you can use a personality profile to discover your own mind-set.

What behavior in yourself do you hate? "What I hate most in myself is the trouble I have enjoying my achievements. I don't seem to have trouble being successful, but I worry whether I have done enough and, as a result, spoil my sense of accomplishment. I also have trouble feeling close to people that I care about. If they have problems, I feel I have to help them, to make sure they do things well. I don't always resent it, but I have difficulty not being helpful, even when this interferes with things I want to do for myself."

Which situations in your life make the behavior you hate worse? "When I do things well, I tend to feel more worried than happy. I don't like to be involved with needy people because I feel obligated to help them. I am intolerant of incompetent or whiny people because they make me feel I have to take care of them."

Which situations in your life make the behavior you hate better? "When I do things well and am appreciated for it, I feel happy and relaxed. I enjoy being involved with people who are accomplished, self-reliant, and interesting. When I think of my friends, or the women I've been seriously involved with, I realize they have all shared these characteristics. I have the most fun with happy, successful people."

Who are your role models, and what qualities did they have? "One of my role models was my cousin, who was self-assured, charming, and effective with people. Very little perturbed him. He was able to be successful without feeling guilty about it. Also, he never seemed self-conscious when he was admired by others. He was unusual to me because, unlike so many people I knew, he had a combination of intellectual talent, social skills, self-assuredness, and integrity."

Do you ever notice yourself treating your children, partner, or others the way you were treated?   "I find that I am a perfectionist with my children and don't have enough patience with their mistakes. I don't remember if that was how I was treated. However, I tend to be stubborn and opinionated with my children like my father was with me. I find that I am provoked by my wife when she is disorganized. It makes me feel that she won't be up to a task and that I will have to take over."

Write a letter to your parents telling them what you wish had been different in your childhood   "Dear Father, you were so depressed about being a failure that you ignored me. I wish you could have been more successful in your life so that we could have been closer. It always bothered me that you constantly worried about money and that you felt you would never be a success. You complained about everything being such a burden for you. This made me feel sorry for you. I felt that you resented my successes because you felt they would diminish your ego. I don't think that you were aware that you always had to be the center of attention. It seemed that you were always changing the subject of conversation to bring it back to yourself. You didn't consider the other person's point of view. That made it very difficult to have a conversation with you."

"Dear Mother, I wish you had been a happier person, who didn't complain so much. Your complaining made me feel as if I had to reassure you all the time to help you feel happier. Also, when I was finished with graduate school, you tried to make me feel guilty about moving away from home. This made it seem that I had to take care of all your problems, even to the point of never leaving home."

SUMMARY

When we evaluate all these answers, it becomes apparent that this man was troubled by two or three major issues. He felt that his mother got most of her satisfaction in life through his achievements, which made him feel he had to perform to make her happy. Accommodating to his mother's needs required him to be perfect, or else he would feel that he was disappointing her. This also made it hard for him to move away from her.

That accounts for his resenting people who are needy, disorganized, or unhappy, because it makes him feel that he has to rescue them. This was reinforced by having to take the place of his parents in caring for his younger brother. He has a hard time tolerating mistakes or shortcomings in his wife and children, because this makes him feel that he has to worry about them and be burdened with responsibility for them (the way he felt growing up).

Because his father was a failure and compensated by acting opinionated and needing to be the center of attention, this man became worried rather than happy when he was achieving. He unconsciously believed that feeling agitated instead of elated when he was successful kept his father from being envious of him. As a result, as an adult he only enjoys being involved with successful, competent, and interesting people who wouldn't be threatened by his successes, and who could therefore appreciate him.

He becomes stubborn and opinionated with his own children, the same way his father was with him. By mimicking his father's traits, he prevents himself from feeling that he is a better parent than his father was. In his unconscious mind, this also serves to keep his father from feeling envious of him. Behaving with his own children the way his father behaved with him also keeps him from remembering how he was treated by his father.

You can learn about your self-defeating motives either by starting with an awareness of the qualities in yourself that you dislike or by examining the worst personality flaws of your family.

If you have completed your personality profiles and used the charts to trace the source of your problems, you will now understand the specific familial cause of your current difficulties. Remember, without knowing that you have hidden self-defeating motives, and without understanding how they specifically affect you, you can't apply conscious efforts to change your behavior. Now that you are clear about your hidden motives, you are able to progress towards your goals.

Let's say that you have made positive changes but at a particular time notice that you are beginning to undo them. At that moment you can scan your life to see if a situation you're in, or if a person you have an important relationship with, is provoking you in ways that are similar to the way you were provoked in your childhood by someone in your family. You will be able to see the connection, realize the irrational effect it is having on you, and as a result overcome it.

Following are two common problems related to the behavior of family members, and how awareness of their origin and effects on you should enable you to overcome them. The information you acquire is similar to learning verbs and their conjugations when you want to learn a foreign language. No matter how badly you may want to speak, it will be impossible to make any progress without knowing these fundamentals.

Just as it is not easy to become fluent in a foreign language, it isn't always easy to act on the new information about the causes of your unwanted behaviors because they have been with you for such a long time. Some of the following examples and suggestions will provide you with some guidelines to help you implement your new knowledge.

Problems with Success

As we have seen, people who have difficulty fulfilling their ambitions or achieving success may believe that they are hurting someone else if they do well. That causes them to feel guilty and therefore undeserving of success. If you notice that success continually eludes you, unless you begin to inquire into the underlying causes you will not be able to overcome the problem. Creating family profiles and using the charts will enable you to see how your accommodations, rebellions, and mimicking, in response to family personality flaws, are responsible for your failings. Here are some examples to illustrate how to further use the information in the book.

Are you behaving in a self-defeating way as a result of mimicking the negative qualities of a parent or sibling? What if your father continually demeaned people in order to feel superior and, without realizing it, you have been doing the same to others? Why repeat the behavior you disliked in him? If you mimic his flawed qualities, you are just like him, and that protects him from experiencing you as superior to him. However, behaving this way will obviously have a negative effect on your business and professional associations. Once you have created his profile, you will be more aware of how his putting others down has influenced you to do the same.

What do you do if, in spite of this new awareness and determination to act differently, you find yourself slipping back into this pattern of demeaning others? After noticing it, observe whether it is taking place with your children, at work, or with your spouse or lover. In which of those situations did your father act the worst? Was it in all of them or mainly with you? Are you doing it to your son? If so, immediately use the awareness to apologize to him. It will not only make you feel better about yourself, but the positive result you get will encourage you to be more alert to not doing it again. You will also feel proud of yourself for finally changing, and that will positively motivate you to do better the next time.

Sometimes you can achieve better clarity by asking yourself, "If someone in my current situation were to ask me how to handle it, what advice would I give?" It will force you to assess the situation more objectively and make it easier to apply the advice to yourself. In the example above "If a friend asked me what to do about the bind he is in with his son as a result of being too critical, what would I advise?" It would be obvious to you that he should apologize. Now follow that advice and do it with your son.

What if your lack of business or professional success is the result of an accommodation to a parent or sibling who was extremely self-centered, insecure, and threatened by and jealous of anyone who was successful and in the limelight? For example, do you overly defer to others, act silly, or make mistakes so that they can feel superior to you? This continuation of the accommodation pattern begun with your parent or sibling is likely to cause others to see you as weak, silly, or inadequate.

Without this knowledge, you would not be able to correct your pattern of acting silly, making mistakes, or overly deferring to others. Now when you get angry with yourself for behaving this way, you can say to yourself, "I know that I am doing this to keep the other person superior. Just because my father required this doesn't mean that my teacher, boss, friend, or any-one else requires it." This enables you to make a conscious effort to be different this time because you know it is not related to the current relationship. As you act more appropriately, you will notice positive responses and increased respect from the person you are interacting with. This will reassure you that the other person is not in fact threatened by you the way your father was. Do you see how conscious awareness of your dynamics can help you overcome your self-defeating behavior?

Do you unnecessarily defy those in positions of authority because you rebelled against a controlling or domineering parent? If so, you will be unable to be flexible and cooperative when requests are made of you by people who may be very influential in your professional life. What do you do if you experienc a teacher, or boss getting angry at you for being uncooperative? Do you dig your heels in or wonder why it is happening again? You now have the answers and can use them to your advantage. You know you have the tendency to be defiant because of your authoritarian parent. Therefore, you can back away, apologize, and correct for your overreaction. Again, you will achieve positive results and positive reinforcement to succeed again.

In contrast with the example above, you may instead discover that you accommodated to a domineering parent, and as a result became too submissive and afraid of asserting yourself. You believed that asserting yourself hurt your parent and assume that it will similarly hurt others. As a result, this may have kept you from routinely speaking up in your own behalf when it was to your advantage. The frustration that you feel from being unassertive should motivate you to investigate this quality in this section of the book. Recognition of the causes of your passivity should allow you to now understand the underlying reasons for your lack of success, relieve your sense of blame, and therefore allow you to become more self-promoting.

Every time you pass up an opportunity to speak up, assert your position, or negotiate from a position of strength, you will feel angry with yourself, but not helpless, because you will be able to recognize it and change it. You will be able to realize that you were unnecessarily holding yourself back because of an irrational worry about hurting the other person. Therefore, you can more clearly prepare yourself for the next negotiation, or improve on the current one. The first steps will make you so proud of yourself that you will be emboldened to continue your new course.

If your mother was overly critical or rejecting when you were charming, you assumed that she was threatened by these qualities. How can you succeed when you are afraid to be engaging with people? Now, armed with the truth, you can see that your parent's rejecting or critical nature had nothing to do with you. Do you see the door opening? You will be in position to see how you limit your effectiveness, realizing that it is your sense of guilt toward your mother that is frustrating your success.

If your parents' well-being depended on your successes—in other words, they lived through your accomplishments—you might have been so afraid of failing and disappointing them that your worry would interfere with your ability to promote your ambition. This is similar to the excessive pressure many children feel from their parents to succeed at all costs in sports or in school. It has the paradoxical effect of causing these children to feel much too anxious to compete successfully.

Now when you find yourself in a competitive situation, you will be able to stop worrying about disappointing someone if you aren't perfect. That will actually free you to perform better than you expect.

Or conversely, if you see that your parents or siblings were envious of or competitive with you, you will understand why today you may keep yourself from being successful in your career and in relationships. When you realize that you have been holding yourself back to protect your parents and siblings from feeling threatened, insecure, or envious, you will feel justified in pursuing success for yourself.

What is the advantage of knowing the truth? As a child, you believed that your parents and/or siblings were victims of some of your normal childhood behaviors and that you were the cause of their pain. Because they acted like the victims of your behavior, you felt like a criminal who should be punished by being made to feel unhappy the same way they were; or you felt that you should appease them by accommodating their flaws; or you felt that you should mimic them in order to not outdo them.

Learning the truth helps you see that, in fact, you were innocent, and therefore that you do not have to undo yourself in your
current life situation.

Problems with Relationships

The same tactics of accommodating, rebelling, and mimicking
that you developed to deal with your family affect your behavior with others in adulthood. Remember, the reason you are
struggling is because your normal childhood behaviors caused
some of your family members to act wounded by them. Therefore you compromised some of your normal behaviors.

Rebelling and protesting against parental behavior can also
be a major cause of undermining your success. You can imagine
how rebelling against an authoritarian parent by becoming antagonistic, defiant, and passiveaggressive would hamper your
success in the world. You might think of your antiauthoritarian
position as a virtue, when in truth it may simply be the result of
needing to rebel against past familial authority. What is the
advantage of knowing the truth? If you are not compelled to take
the opposite point of view and can genuinely agree with someone else when it fits with your values, you are a truly independent
person.

Can you see how rebelling against a cold or rejecting parent can cause you to always require getting attention or to insist
on having your demands met? How will that attitude help you to
achieve success when it can so easily undermine your interactions with people?

If your parent was overly righteous and moralistic and you
rebel by getting into trouble or by having moral failures, it is
likely to undermine your best intentions to be successful.

By now you may realize how difficult it is to know the truth. This
is why it's crucial to create personality profiles for you and your
family to see what hidden mechanisms affect the way you relate
to people. The profiles and the charts can make you see clearly
what happened in the past and how those events are affecting
your life in the present.

Here is an example. If you feel responsible for re
everyone you think is unhappy, you may not be able to resist
requests or demands made by others. As a result, you are likely
to feel angry with yourself for getting taken advantage of. Your
dilemma is probably the result of becoming vulnerable to making excessive sacrifices for a family member you felt sorry for.

Look at the chart Checking Out Your Symptoms and
locate your problem with rescuing people. The chart will help
you to understand which parental flaw caused your accommodation. Once you examine your past and realize that a particular
family member's unhappiness was not your fault, you will realize that you deserve to do better for yourself. You have been
released from psychological jail. Every time that you notice yourself acting too self-sacrificing toward someone in your current
life, you will be able to use your new knowledge to realize that
you are repeating a pattern from the past that does not currently
apply.

You may find yourself angry for not asserting yourself and
not immediately realize that you are too worried about making
the other person feel unhappy. What do you do? Let your anger
be a signal to you that you have again been too self-sacrificing.
Ask yourself why you are doing this now. Is your spouse or lover
currently acting victimized? Ask yourself, "If someone else who
was a rescuer asked me what to do about his or her current self-
sacrifice, how would I evaluate it and advise him or her?" Now
apply the advice to your own situation.

What if you realize that you avoid getting close to a spouse
or lover, or create distance by having affairs. You want to change
but don't understand what prevents you from achieving your
goal.

Was it because your parent was rejecting and you fear rejection? Were you used as a child and, as a result, fear being manipulated? Did you have a parent who vicariously lived through
your sexual conquests causing you to continuously have affairs
in order to make them happy?

Instead, was your parent overly possessive towards you so
that you fear feeling trapped if you let yourself feel close to
someone? Is that your motive for having affairs instead of letting

yourself get close to one person? Was your parent too moralistic about sex, causing you to rebel by having a promiscuous lifestyle? Are you minsinterpreting your partner's interest in monogamy with your parent's excessive moralizing about sex? Or are you mimicking a parent who was forever having affairs, thereby preventing yourself from having greater intimacy?

Do you see how important it is to recognize the dynamic that applies so that you can begin to accurately think about the motivations for your current problems?

What if you discover that the reason for keeping distant is to protect against the fear of being trapped by an overly possessive parent, and in the process of making this assessment you realize that your spouse or lover doesn't act possessively towards you? This should help you to distinguish between the trapped feeling you felt in relation to your parent's need for you and the sincere interest your spouse or lover may have in you. What can you do?

Discuss this with your partner so he or she won't be unnecessarily offended by the distance you created between the two of you. Bringing it out in the open is another way of getting control over your anxiety about closeness. It will also help your partner not to feel rejected, and therefore not need to have additional reassurance from you. Remember, because of your experience with your possessive parent, any pull for reassurance and love tends to arouse your worry about being sucked in and trapped.

Or, if you realize that your problem with intimacy is related to having been rejected by your parents and that you worry about being rejected again, this may help you to be less standoffish with your spouse or lover. Again, discuss it openly.

If you know that you are compelled to say no to requests because you were made to give in to an authoritarian or controlling parent as a child, it may help you understand that agreeing with your spouse does not mean that you are weak. Ask yourself whether your partner's requests are reasonable. If a friend were to tell you that his or her spouse was making those requests, would you think them reasonable or not? Your improved perspective should help you to feel freer to say no or yes when you mean it and to not assume that you are wrong or hurting someone else just for having an independent point of view.

You are unhappy about having been told over and over that you are cold or insensitive to suffering and have learned that you developed that trait as a rebellion against having to take care of a long-suffering parent. (See the movie *Marvin's Room* wtih Meryl Streep.) There is an important difference between the long-term suffering of a parent or sibling and the transient upsets that everyone goes through. The personality profiles will help you distinguish between the two. Again, try discussing it with your spouse or lover.

It may shock you to discover that you treat your children, spouse, pets, friends, and colleagues the way that you were treated by your parents. In other words, you are mimicking behavior that you vowed to forever avoid! Because you think you caused that behavior in others, you feel that you must behave the same way as a form of punishment. Or you may be protecting your parent or sibling by mimicking them instead of outdoing them.

It should be a relief for you to realize that what you do to others is not always provoked by their behavior toward you. As a result, your relationships with others should improve.

CHAPTER TWELVE

Problems with Your Children

Perhaps you've realized by now that you have spent much of your life in psychological jail. Self-blame locked you in. Until you realized that you were innocent of the crime, you couldn't open the door.

What about your children? Have they also been locked in a psychological jail because of you? If so, you may be able to help them open the door. To do so you'll have to look for clues as to why they are imprisoned.

Clues to Look for

You may notice that your children repeatedly behave with you in ways that you find provocative. Why do they do so in spite of the angry, critical responses they receive from you? This is a case in which negative reinforcement from you doesn't produce positive results in your child, but it does provide you with something useful. You are being signaled to evaluate and change your behavior with your child.

Why do children continue to act in ways that elicit negative responses from their parents instead of doing what will make their parents happy? *It is because they are experiencing unpleasant or painful interactions with you and are communicating it to you through behavior, not words.* For example, has anyone ever heard a five- or ten- year-old say to his or her parent, "Your behavior is undermining my psychosocial development"?

Let's examine what their provocative behavior is about. One explanation is that their parents have been behaving with them in a way that is unpleasant for them, and now they are returning the favor by doing it back to their parents. For example, if you have been cold or rejecting, your child in return acts cold or rejecting toward you. Why are they mimicking you? They not only want you to change your behavior but also want to see if you can manage to stay calm and unprovoked when criticized so that they can learn from you how to be calm when criticized too.

A second motive for acting provocatively with you is to rebel as a protest against what they don't like about your behavior. They want you to understand this form of communication and use it to take action. This should be the signal to use what you have already learned about yourself and change your behavior. In the past you probably gave in to negative emotions when provoked by your children. Now you have a new understanding. Instead of automatically blaming them and getting angry, try using your personality profile to see how you may have contributed to the problem. Ask yourself, "Have I been acting this way with them because that is how my parents behaved with me?" "Are my actions with them a result of accommodation or rebellion in relation to my parents when I was a child?" Once you understand your motives, you will be able to shift your attitude. You will realize that the problem with your child is a result of your actions, and therefore can be overcome.

A third reason you feel upset can paradoxically be your child's attempt at pleasing you. I will explain more about that later in the chapter.

Take Criticism . . . Please!

For example, if, without being aware of it, you have been excessively critical of your children the way your parents were toward you, your children may begin to criticize you unreasonably.

Again, the purpose of this behavior is to get you to stop being so critical because the situation is unpleasant for them.

Why don't they simply tell you to stop criticizing them as opposed to criticizing you in turn? Some children do. But remember, self-blame may have your children locked in psychological jail. If so, you can help them open the door.

Your children may have developed destructive mind-sets and acquired behavior you hate in response to your criticism. This may have led them to mimic your behavior.

Unconsciously, they also want to see if you can show them that you are now unprovoked by criticism. If you can demonstrate for them that you are not easily distressed, are not defensive, and can remain composed in the face of their criticism, you will become an effective role model. In other words, you will have demonstrated to them how to not become agitated when criticized. In this way you will help them overcome their problem in dealing with your criticism. (This equally applies to over-possessiveness, rejection, neediness, authoritarianism, and other kinds of negative behavior.)

If you become angry at your children for criticizing you, your negative reaction will not necessarily stop their criticism. Your children will interpret your anger as your inability to face criticism. They will continue to be critical until you demonstrate how to respond to their negativity in a matter-of-fact way.

Another reason they mimic you is that they blame themselves for causing your critical attitude. Therefore, their feelings of guilt require them to suffer from the same defect that they think they caused you to have. This is their way of atoning. They made you unhappy and are now required to be unhappy too.

What will make it difficult for you to control your anger? Of course, your lack of awareness about how you were hurt by your own parents' criticism causes you to be overly sensitive to criticism from your children. Thus, when your children criticize you, you become as reactive and angry as if your parents were criticizing you all over again.

Stop and think for a minute. If you still haven't resolved the hurt you experienced with your parents, how can you handle the same hurt you are now experiencing with your children?

A Second Chance to Break the Cycle

The first step to gaining control over this problem is to accept that the way you are reacting to your children is not helping to change their behavior. Whatever you've tried hasn't worked, has it?

The second thing to do is to check your family personality profiles to verify whether your parents behaved the same way with you. If so, you may feel less provoked when your children behave this way. You may even feel challenged to behave better with your child than your parent did with you. *You will realize that you are part of a cycle that can be broken. The most important proof of your success is the improvement in your children's behavior.*

The purpose of their negative behavior is to get control over an unpleasant situation. In a sense, they are giving you a second chance to deal with your problem. If you are unprovoked by their behavior with you and you deal with it in an appropriate way, it models for them a better way of dealing with you. It also shows you how you might have responded if your parents had handled you correctly. This helps to diminish self-blame.

So far we've looked at how your children may be provocative by doing to you what you did to them. But, as we all know, there are other ways they may behave in response to you.

YOUR CHILDREN MAY REBEL AGAINST YOUR BEHAVIOR

This you will probably find equally provocative. When you examine the chart at the end of this chapter called Problems with Your Children (pages 163–165), you will notice in the third column a group of rebellious conduct that may include some of the behaviors you hate. For example, instead of criticizing you in response to being criticized, they might deny your accusations and refuse to listen to any suggestions or comments you make. This can make you feel very frustrated and angry.

If you are a perfectionist, they might become sloppy, careless, do poorly in school, and refuse to compete. If you are too controlling, they will probably be defiant and stubborn. If your attitude about sex or drugs is too rigid, you may see rebellious promiscuity or excessive drug use. If you need them to be close to you (too possessive), they will maintain emotional distance from you and keep their personal lives secret. If you are too self-centered, they will avoid giving you credit for your accomplishments. If you are too moralistic and righteous about a particular subject, that will most likely be the area in which they get into trouble. If you always give in to them because you have an excessive need to be liked, they will push you to stand up to them. If you are indifferent or uncaring, they will demand attention by acting in an outlandish way, or by acting very needy. If you are overprotective, they will expose themselves to dangerous situations.

If you are unclear about the rebellious behavior you are observing, go to the chart Problems with Your Children and locate your child's behavior. That will inform you what it is about you that they are rebelling against and enable you to focus on how it developed in your own family so that you can change it.

YOUR CHILDREN MAY ACCOMMODATE TO YOUR BEHAVIOR

This may cause you to feel terribly disappointed with them. For example, if in response to your being critical of them your children act withdrawn or accept your negative opinions of them ("I'm no good," "I'm lazy," "I'm selfish," "I'm rotten," and so on), you may not respect them, even though they are simply trying to accommodate to you! Ask yourself, "Are they just responding to my critical nature?" If you are overprotective, you may find yourself feeling frustrated about having such a cautious child, which inhibits him or her from participating in sports. If you are underprotective, you will probably be provoked when your child becomes a daredevil or exposes himself to unnecessary danger.

Again, the most important guide is their behavior. *If you change your attitude toward your children and their behavior improves, it means that you are doing right by them. Conversely, if their behavior stays the same or gets worse, you need to figure out what you need to change in yourself.*

It is often helpful to compare how your children relate to your partner in contrast with yourself. You may notice that a particular behavior of your children that upsets you is not provocative to your partner. Likewise, when your partner wonders why you are so provoked by certain situations, this should also stimulate curiosity in you about the cause of your reactions. These are useful clues that you have a heightened sensitivity to your children's behavior because of experiences you had with your parents.

Many parents wonder if their children were simply born with the tendency to behave badly. They believe that they have done everything right with their children. It never occurs to them that their children's actions may be a direct response to their parents' behavior. When parents see that their children react to the same situation that oppressed the parents in their childhood, it can help free both parents and children.

A Look at Bossiness

If you or your partner are acting bossy towards your children, you may notice them acting bossy towards you. Again, one purpose is to see if you are unprovoked by bossiness. If, for example, when your children are bossy you can calmly explain that you disagree with their point of view, this should help to diminish their bossiness over time. The same principle applies to rejection, possessiveness, competitiveness, and so on.

If, instead, your children are rebelling or protesting against your authoritarian or controlling attitude, they will refuse to do what you ask or demand of them. They will do it either in an openly defiant way or in a more subtle passive-aggressive way, such as by forgetting to do things that are expected of them. When you understand what the protest is about and you diminish your controlling behavior towards them, their defiant behavior will begin to ease.

If in response to your being controlling they accommodate to you by being meek, overly obedient, or a "goody two shoes," ironically you may find yourself being upset by their lack of defiance.

A Brief Word About Adolescence

The turmoil that adolescents experience reflects the conflict they have about their need to reject and become independent of their

PROBLEMS WITH YOUR CHILDREN

What You Do to Them	They Do to You What You Did to Them	They Rebel or Protest	They Accommodate
You are critical of them.	They are critical of you.	They deny your accusations and refuse to listen to your suggestions.	They accept your criticisms and accuse themselves. "I'm selfish, no good, lazy, rotten, dishonest, etc."
You are perfectionistic with them. You live through their accomplishments.	They are perfectionistic with you. In their eyes you always fall short.	They are sloppy, careless, and may refuse to compete.	They are driven to succeed but anxious when performing (fear of failure).
You are controlling and authoritarian.	They are controlling and demanding with you.	They are defiant, rebellious, and passive-aggressive.	They are submissive, obedient, and meek.
You act rejecting of them.	They reject you.	They demand attention at any cost to themselves.	They control their feelings of need for affection.
You are possessive of them.	They are possessive towards you.	They stay away from you and keep emotional distance from you.	They cling to you and have trouble leaving home (school phobia).
You are depressed or needy with them.	They are depressed and needy around you.	They are indifferent to complaints or suffering.	They are overly attentive to you. They go overboard to make you happy.

What You Do to Your Children	Your Children Do to You What You Did to Them	Your Children Rebel or Protest	Your Children Accommodate
You are focused on yourself and have to be the center of attention.	They are self-centered and focus attention on themselves.	They never give you credit for your accomplishments.	They stay in the background and avoid showing what they can do.
You are submissive and usually give in.	They are submissive and give in.	They are stubborn and refuse to give in.	They take charge and make decisions for you.
You are abusive to them.	They are abusive towards you or others.	If possible, they fight back. They become rebellious and antisocial.	They become fearful, withdrawn, sullen, depressed, or spaced out.
You are shy.	They are shy.	They take center stage.	They try to bring you out.
You are overprotective.	They express an extreme worry about you getting hurt.	They take unnecessary chances and expose themselves to danger. They are known as daredevils.	They become overly cautious about sports and other activities. They worry about getting injured.
You are underprotective.	They ignore you when you or their siblings are in danger; for example, if you are drunk and want to go for a drive.	They become overly cautious and can't easily have fun.	They take chances and expose themselves to danger.

You are dishonest in your dealings with people.	They lie, cheat, and steal excessively.	They become overly concerned with doing the right thing, to the point of moral righteousness.	They have trouble following the rules and doing right by people.
You are righteous and disdainful of others.	They act morally superior to you and point out your faults.	They will highlight their failures, get into trouble, and become antisocial.	They will highlight their virtues and act contemptous of others.
You abuse drugs and alcohol. You may be unreliable, unpredictable, and/or violent.	They abuse drugs, become erratic, unreliable, and possibly violent.	They act hateful towards you or anyone on drugs and not in control. They may become insensitive to suffering in others.	They become vigilant and alert and act parental towards you. They feel anxious and inhibit themselves to avoid setting you off.

parents. As a result, many teenagers have a tendency to feel guilty about these strivings. These feelings of guilt become more difficult for them to master, if, all through their childhood, their parents behaved towards them in many of the ways I have discussed.

For example, they will experience more conflict about wanting independence if their parent has been authoritarian and controlling. Therefore, you may see more passive-aggressive forms of defiance such as sneaking out at night, lying about their plans, and keeping secret their sexual activity and use of drugs. If, instead, you are surprised about how good your teenager is compared to his or her friends, it may be a sign of over-compliance with your need to be in control.

A possessive parent will cause adolescents to experience intensified guilt about forming close relationships both with peers and the opposite sex. If you notice that they pursue people who don't reciprocate their interest, these rejections may serve to help them atone for feelings of disloyalty to you. On the other hand, if they rebel against your possessiveness, you may notice extreme emotional distance from you.

If you have been overprotective, it will cause them to be too cautious, and as a result interfere with their struggle to be independent. On the other hand, they may rebel by routinely exposing themselves to danger, causing you to feel great anxiety.

If you are depressed and needy, they will feel obligated to be very attentive to you. As a result, you may notice that they have difficulty feeling happy. Rebelling is likely to take the form of indifference to suffering in others.

If you are dishonest in your dealings with others, it may cause them to have difficulty doing right by people. If you notice that your child has an excessive concern with moral righteousness, it is probably a rebellion against your behavior.

In addition, there are other qualities in you that can easily intensify the conflicts that adolescents experience. If you feel competitive with them, or see yourself as the enlightened authority confronted by a know-it-all attitude, or tend to feel overwhelmed by turmoil, you may have difficulty coping with the changes taking place in your children.

In Closing

Now look at the accompanying chart, Problems with Your Children, to help you recognize your behavioral patterns. The first column describes your behavior. The next column describes the kind of behavior your children do to you because you have been doing it to them.

The third column describes how your children may rebel against you. For example, if you are a perfectionist, they will rebel against the requirement to be perfect at all costs to themselves. Therefore, you will notice behavior such as excessive sloppiness, making poor grades, and refusing to compete.

The last column shows examples of accommodation to your expectations. For example, if you are a perfectionist, your children may be driven to succeed and feel very anxious when performing because of their fear of failing you. As a result, either they will fail consistently, or they will succeed but not enjoy their success. A good example is a child athlete such as a gymnast or an ice skater whose life has no meaning outside of the few moments he or she spends performing. Another is the one-dimensional child whose life is nothing without perfect grades.

Finally, you may see combinations of these adaptations in your children, which can be confusing. Don't let this throw you. Because giving in to you makes them feel resentful, they will sometimes shift to a rebellious attitude. Then, conversely, since rebellious behavior makes them feel guilty, they may shift back to accommodation.

Remember, the reason you may feel especially provoked and disturbed by your children's accommodation and/or rebellious behavior is that it reminds you of how you adapted to your parents' problems. The surface manifestation is your anger. What is hidden beneath your anger are your own painful experiences with your parents, which caused you to inhibit your personal fulfillment as a result of accommodating, rebelling, and mimicking.

CHAPTER THIRTEEN

Can Psycho-therapy Succeed Where Your Parents Failed?

IF YOU FEEL THAT WHAT YOU HAVE learned about yourself thus far has been valuable, but you still think that you need additional help, you may decide to seek psychotherapy. For most people, what takes place in psychotherapy is mysterious. Yet many people pursue this process to solve their personal problems. How can therapy help you to change when your willpower can't? It is much less mysterious and complicated than most people think.

If you have a self-destructive mind-set, you view the world based on a specific set of hidden expectations and dictates. Therefore, you will have difficulty navigating through life, because you will create obstacles instead of solutions. Unless you uncover and dispel your mind-set, you may be inclined to see many experiences in life as threatening. Your adaptations to your parents' and/or siblings' deficiencies have given you a distorted view of the world. In therapy, your goal is to correct your vision so you can see the world more clearly. How can you accomplish this goal?

Remember how in the highway close call the driver successfully faced the danger? He only allowed himself to experience anxiety when the situation had passed and he was safely parked. In therapy, as in your personal relationships, you need to feel safe before you can risk exposing yourself to feelings, memories, and behavior that your mind-set defines as dangerous. Otherwise, you will be unable to face your troubled past, recognize its unfortunate impact on your life, and get control over it.

How can you assure yourself that you will feel safe during therapy? You will have to assess the qualities of your therapist. We will see how accommodation, rebellion, and mimicking are crucial to this goal.

The First Date

How do we learn how other people feel about us? Often, especially with a new acquaintance, we may try out different kinds of behavior such as shyness, bravado, joking, teasing, seriousness, reticence, or questioning to see how the other person responds.

We want to feel reassured that it will be safe to get more involved or to learn whether it is best to keep our distance. You might act towards a date the way your parents or siblings did with you, to see how resilient your date is. With a therapist, you want to assess his or her good and bad qualities, just as you would with anyone else. But in this case it's doubly important to be sure that you can be helped and not be hurt by him or her. I will describe how you accomplish this.

Learning that your therapist has motivations and attitudes that are different than your parents' makes you more secure to be yourself in therapy instead of behaving as you were compelled to with your parents. This also frees you to remember your past bad experiences with your parents. Once you are secure, you can remember a time when you were insecure and how it affected you.

If, for example, your therapist is supportive of your desire for success when your parents weren't, that will make it easier for you to be more successful. It will also allow you to remember a time when your desires for success were undermined, and to see how your parents' past attitudes are still currently influencing your ability to achieve success in your life.

The desire to change is so vital to your well-being that it is crucial for your therapist to be receptive to the goals you have for yourself and to understand how your parents' behavior kept you from achieving those goals. It is also essential that when you behave with your therapist as your parent did with you that your therapist is able to deal with it better than you were. If you can learn from your therapist how to face what was unpleasant in your childhood, it will make it easier for you to remember what you have hidden.

My Therapist, My Parent?

Accommodating, rebelling, and mimicking, the three methods of coping that we have been discussing throughout this book, are, surprisingly enough, also crucial to the success or failure of your psychotherapy. Without being aware of it, you will probably behave toward your therapist in one or more of these three ways, as you did with your parents and siblings. What are your unconscious motives for this behavior, and how does it work?

Remember, it is crucial that your therapist possess attitudes and views that are different from those in your parents that caused your problems. To verify this, you must probe the attitudes and beliefs of your therapist. Doing so has the following benefits: (1) You can avoid the risk of being hurt or misdirected by your therapist, and (2) you can ascertain that your therapist is not vulnerable to being hurt by you.

There are many examples of this. For instance, if your parent was critical, it is most important that your therapist be understanding. If your parent was rigid, it will be important that your therapist be flexible. If your parent was self-centered and competitive with you, it will be important that your therapist not be threatened by your success, allowing you to feel proud of yourself and not become defensive or critical if you criticize him or her.

If your parent was possessive, it will be important that your therapist not need you and feel comfortable and not jealous when you focus on the importance of other people in your life. If your parent lived through your accomplishments, it will be crucial that your therapist not act hurt if you are disappointed in how the therapy is going, or if you credit changes in your life to factors outside of therapy.

If your parent was unprotective of you, it will be essential that your therapist warn you and, if necessary, intervene if you exhibit self-destructive behavior. In all these cases, the therapist needs to correct for the bad traits of your parents or siblings. In other words, the therapist needs to make safe what was dangerous. Here is an example of how a client learned whether I possessed an attitude that was important to him.

Jeremy's father cheated people, including members of his family. As a result of his father's dishonesty, Jeremy was uncomfortable about being honest, because he was uncomfortable feeling morally superior to his father. As a result of Jeremy's conflicted feelings about honesty, it was very important for him to find out whether I had integrity so that he could feel more comfortable being honest himself.

His strategy involved paying my bill in cash. I didn't understand why he did this, so I asked if he paid all his bills that way. He said no, but that he had received some money from a foreign investment and wanted to use it to pay my bill. The implication was that he was asking me to be involved in something shady. How could I respond?

I had two possibilities: to either accept the cash or ask him instead to pay by check. Remember, I was dealing both with his conflicted feelings about honesty as well as how he would judge me by my response.

If Jeremy took my request for payment by check to mean that I didn't trust him, he might be angry. But if he took my position to mean that I was affirming his honesty, he would be relieved. His explanation about the foreign investment seemed odd, so I asked him to pay by check. He didn't complain at all, but simply took out his checkbook to pay me.

In the next session he revealed for the first time the story of his father's dishonesty. I soon learned that Jeremy's investments and business dealings had always been aboveboard. Since he felt guilty about being superior to his dishonest father, he found it difficult to reveal to me and others that he was honest.

One of Jeremy's goals was to learn how to feel at ease about being honest in his dealings with people. As his therapist, I could help him reach his goals only after passing his test for honesty. He didn't have to accommodate to me as he had to his father, so now he was free to demonstrate his integrity. His father had made it dangerous for Jeremy to be honest. By passing his test, I reassured him that my attitude made it safe for him to promote his goal.

THIS IS A TEST

You may be surprised to learn that you have an amazing capacity to unconsciously test your therapist to see if he or she will behave like your parents or siblings. But if you think about it, this makes sense. All your life you've had to adapt to the extreme pressures of your parents' behavior via accommodation, rebellion, self-blame, and mimicking. You've become very adept at judging and assessing behavior, even in someone other than a family member.

It is essential that your therapist has the correct qualities; otherwise, you will not be able to see what causes you to behave in ways you hate. Does your therapist have the attitudes and motivations that will help you to learn about your hidden mind-sets? Will he or she enable you to face the behavior you hate in yourself as well as the source of it in your painful memories?

One of my clients always credited her exercise program and a relationship with a close friend for the changes that had taken place in her life since she began therapy with me. Unconsciously, she hoped that I would not be hurt by not being credited with helping her, as her parent would have been. By testing me she became reassured of my lack of neediness and was freer to be independent with me.

Assessing your therapist's qualities involves learning about how he or she will deal with you when you employ the three coping mechanisms of accommodation, rebellion, and mimicking in your therapy. It involves the following:

1. Evaluating how he or she responds to you when you accommodate to what you think he or she expects of you.
2. Assessing his or her responses when you rebel against the assumed expectations.
3. Learning about the way he or she deals with your doing to them what your parents and siblings did to you.

Here is a brief example. If as a child you were rejected by your mother, you will test your therapist to learn if your therapist is also rejecting. You might make overtures such as being friendly or humorous to see if he or she responds in a positive or negative way. You might expose a minor flaw to ascertain if your therapist will overlook it or criticize it. Here is how it worked with a female client of mine.

Frieda, a middle-aged woman, had a very rejecting mother, who didn't want her daughter around. When Frieda was with her mother, her mother would shut her up whenever Frieda tried to express her point of view. The adage "Children should be seen but not heard" was changed in her case to "be not seen and not heard."

Early in therapy with me, Frieda failed to show up for several appointments and was relieved when I called her. She was relieved because it demonstrated to her that, unlike her mother, I was interested in her and wanted her around.

If, instead of being rejecting, Frieda's mother had been possessive, not wanting her to be involved with other people, Frieda would probably have experienced my calling her differently. Instead of feeling relieved, she would have been upset because it would have signified to her that I was possessive the way her mother was. In other words, I needed her to be with me.

BEHAVING TOWARD YOUR THERAPIST AS YOU DID WITH YOUR PARENTS

When You Accommodate   The purpose of accommodation is to find out if your therapist will treat you as your family members did. Perhaps you were required by your parents or siblings to put aside your feelings and goals in order to do what they wanted. Will your therapist require the same? Your hope is that he or she instead will allow you to be yourself. Doing so will help you more clearly see the behavior from your parents or siblings that required you to accommodate.

Suppose you try to please your therapist all the time, and he or she enjoys it, encourages it, or never questions it. Wouldn't you assume he or she is just like the people in your family that you had to please? Of course! Therefore, you will have difficulty not accommodating to your therapist and recognizing the problems in your life that are caused by your accommodating qualities.

If you are a very accommodating person as a result of going along with overbearing parents, how can you recognize their influence on you if your therapist acts similarly? A therapist who is controlling, rigid, or authoritarian in relation to your coming on time, keeping your appointments, and paying your bill, but inflexible about changing appointment times will only reinforce your problems with submission and obedience.

If your mother was possessive of you, and your therapist, in a possessive way, is upset when you cancel sessions or when you compliment other therapists or treatments, it will be difficult for you to remember your mother's possessive attitude towards you and the way it adversely affected your life.

On the other hand, if your therapist questions your accommodating behavior or interprets it, you will feel freer to be yourself and recall the situations in your past that required you to be submissive.

Do you recall Ronald, the dynamic businessman in Chapter Two, whose mother experienced her fulfillment in life through his accomplishments and her relationship with him? It left him with chronic resentment about having to please others without regard to his own needs. He experienced strong guilt feelings when he separated from her, causing him to suffer symptoms as punishment. When he left home at the age of twenty-six, he experienced chest pains after crossing the Mississippi River because it meant there was no turning back. In order to overcome his problems with accommodation, he needed to know if I had expectations of him similar to those of his mother. How did he find out?

One method involved expressing mixed emotions about my occasional note taking, which had been ongoing from the very beginning.

"How do you feel about it?" I asked.

"Well, on the one hand I like it. It makes me feel that you're interested in me. But I also feel burdened by the need to be interesting for you," he said.

"In what way?" I asked.

"It's like being interviewed by a reporter who has an agenda. I don't want to disappoint you."

"What would it be like for you if I stopped taking notes?" I asked.

"Oh," he said. "It wouldn't make a difference. I feel obligated to make the sessions interesting and worthwhile for you either way."

I pointed out that his responses to me were still being governed by his childhood experiences with his mother, which made it difficult for him to assess whether my interest in him was authentic or based on an agenda that mainly served me. Since I had explored what it would be like for him if I stopped taking notes, he realized that he didn't need to please me. Explaining to him how his destructive mind-sets affected his experiences with me and others helped him to feel less concerned about having to accommodate to me. This freed him to develop greater insight into his tendency to accommodate.

He said, "I can only relax when no one is around. Otherwise, I'm always supposed to be on, performing, fulfilling the needs of others. My mother said I was perfect. So I never had an adolescence. I went from baby to adult."

I asked him, "Was there a part of your childhood when you didn't feel you had to be perfect?"

"I liked the Boy Scouts," he said. "To advance you were rated by your peers, as opposed to at school or home where you were judged by authority figures. Authority figures only rewarded you if you fulfilled their expectations. I think that's why I developed a disdain for authority."

You can see from this example how your therapist can help you overcome your problem with accommodation through interpretation and behavior. What if your therapist fails you? This would reinforce your obligation to continue accommodating, and there would be no improvement in your behavior or understanding of its origins. As a result, you may become increasingly resentful and begin to rebel or protest by showing disdain for authority.

When You Rebel   Rebellious behavior means insisting on doing the opposite of what is expected of you, even if you know rationally that it makes no sense. In order to test your therapist's tolerance, you may rebel against what you think he or she expects, then assess how provoked he or she becomes. You will feel less threatened by your obligation to accommodate if your therapist can tolerate a certain amount of rebellion or protest. If your therapist is provoked, that will make you feel more guilty than you already were. If he or she is accepting of and tolerant of your rebellious attitude, or notices your discomfort about it, you will feel more comfortable facing the behavior in your parents and/or siblings that you felt you had to rebel or protest against.

For example, if you had controlling or authoritarian parents or siblings who expected excessive submission, obedience, or compliance to unpleasant demands, you might test your therapist by acting rebellious. Perhaps you will fail to pay your bill on time, or come late, or you might refuse to talk about whatever you think he or she expects you to say. If you are able to be somewhat noncompliant with your therapist, you will be reassured that you can protect yourself from excessive submission and obedience.

This in turn will help you to remember your parents' or siblings' authoritarian behavior and the ways in which you had to accommodate to them. It may also help you see how your rebelliousness caused you to be self-defeating in life.

Do you remember Will, the businessman in Chapter Seven, whose wife could never get him to say yes? Both parents had excessively subjected him to their needs and so oppressed his autonomy. His rebellious behavior had become so self-defeating that he couldn't say yes even when it was reasonable to do so.

Will's problem was similar to that of a businessman named Dana, who became caught in a cycle of rebellion and accommodation. Dana's major successes and, ironically, his major problems in life resulted from his ability to be very pleasing to people (accommodating). Although this enabled him to be very effective with his clients, who enjoyed his interest in them, it simultaneously caused Dana to unconsciously feel resentful that he was so over solicitous of others. In response to this, he would ignore his clients for periods of time in order to prove to himself that he wasn't dominated by his need to please them (rebellion).

Although this behavior was obviously self-defeating because it undermined the goodwill he had achieved by being accommodating to his clients' needs, it was difficult for him to refocus on his clients until a crisis unfolded. His response to their complaints was to again become very attentive to them, act apologetic, and leave them with the impression that he was truly a man of good will. You can see from this example that Dana was caught in a conflict between accommodation and rebellion.

In his therapy, Dana displayed exactly the same behavior he had learned with his parents and later used with his clients. He was charming, engaging, and attentive to anything I had to say (accommodation). This alternated with behavior such as arriving late and missing sessions because of business appointments, for which he was profusely apologetic (rebellion).

One day I noticed his discomfort and inquired, "Why are you so uncomfortable about coming late or missing sessions?" His relief was obvious.

He said, "I was concerned that you would be disappointed in me. I felt worried that you might think I wasn't conscientious or appreciative."

As a result of my noncritical and tolerant attitude, it became safe for Dana to remember the demands his mother had placed on him to be solicitous of her needs and to make her happy by living his life according to her values. He learned in therapy how his mother's requirements of him had made him resentful and rebellious, and how these feelings had carried over to his relationships with me, his clients, and others.

Also, because I didn't demand that Dana arrive on time, discuss what he thought I expected, or never miss an appointment, he could more freely learn what he himself wanted to do.

If Dana could safely be rebellious with me, he could feel free to serve his clients without resenting it and feeling the need to rebel. He showed further evidence of progress in his negotiations with a business associate who made new requests of him. Dana recognized that his initial negative reaction was similar to how he felt about his mother's requests of him. As a result of that insight, he felt freer to more objectively consider the merits of his associate's position and eventually to agree to it. Dana learned to move beyond accommodating and rebellion and into living according to his needs and desires.

So far we have been talking about accommodating to and rebelling against your therapist in relation to important themes in your life that you want to overcome—in other words, putting your therapist in the role your parents or siblings occupied. In this way, you can assess whether he or she has the same expectations of you that your parents or siblings did when you accommodated and/or rebelled as a child.

BAITING THE TRAP

In your unconscious attempts to assess your therapist, you may exert an emotional pull on him or her to act like your parents or siblings, while hoping that he or she won't.

On one level, this is a risky maneuver because your therapist might indeed give in to the temptation you create. This would cause you to suffer again as you did in childhood and to retreat from your goal. But if your therapist is able to overcome the strong temptation to act like your parents or siblings, it will be powerfully reassuring to you that he or she is reliable, resilient, and trustworthy, in ways your parent wasn't. You will know for certain that your therapist is not motivated to behave towards you the way your parents or siblings did.

In the long run, it is less risky for you to find out about your therapist's reliability early in therapy, when you are less vulnerable emotionally. Towards that end, if early on you tempt him or her to fail you in minor ways, you don't risk too much. Dana engaged in this assessment of me in the beginning by coming just a few minutes late for each session to see if I was angry, hurt, or disappointed, the way he would expect his mother to be. He was testing the waters.

After all, in everyday life we often assess the intentions of others. With a potential partner, for example, we might unconsciously act standoffish, sarcastic, or provocative, not because we want to be rejected, but in order to evaluate that person's interest in us. If he or she is not put off by our behavior, it reassures us about that person's interest in us and makes us feel more comfortable about showing our true feelings. Flirting serves the purpose of feeling out the other person's attitudes and interest. It also enables us to take small steps that demonstrate our interest in the other person without risking too much.

We use these methods in other areas of life as well. At work, we might use several strategies to carefully assess our boss's attitudes about us before asking for a raise or disagreeing with him or her.

Let's look at an incident in which such a strategy was used by Frank, a client who had a needy, possessive mother. Frank's mother's behavior made him feel excessively obligated to be with her and to meet all of her requests. He expected the same thing to happen in his other relationships. Therefore, to protect himself from the obligation to fulfill requests, Frank maintained very superficial relationships with people. He feared that if he became too emotionally involved with someone, he would lose his independence as a result of being obligated to them.

Frank devised a strategy to see if I, like his mother, was possessive of him. After we had been working successfully on his problems, he told me that he was going to interview another therapist. The purpose of his apparent ingratitude was to bait a trap for me.

The emotional pull on me to act hurt, like his mother, was risky for Frank, but it was an important test. If I was hurt and angry about his consulting with someone else, it would mean to him that I was possessive and needy of him like his mother was. Conversely, if I could resist being angry with him, it would powerfully reassure him that he could overcome the problems caused by his possessive mother.

I was provoked by Frank's behavior! But I realized the significance of what he was doing and why he was making me angry. Instead of showing him that I was disappointed and hurt, like his mother, I asked him how he felt about telling me his plans. He said he wondered if his seeing another therapist would hurt my feelings.

By overcoming the temptation Frank exerted on me to act like his possessive mother, he felt reassured that I wasn't possessive myself. Now he began to recall instances of his mother's possessiveness. For example, he remembered that she worried excessively that he would be physically hurt and so caused him to restrict his playing with friends. Frank's mind-set was "Mother feels rejected by me, so I'd better stay more involved with her."

His experience with me helped Frank to understand that his feelings of resentment at being obliged to me and others were irrational because they were associated with his childhood experiences of obligation to his mother. That helped him gain more control over his worry that if he felt closer to others he would feel excessively obligated to meet their needs. This was helpful in his relationship with his girlfriend. As a result of being reassured about his ability to distance himself from me when he wanted to, he felt freer to be closer to her. This meant that he could also distance himself from her when he needed to. Closeness with his girlfriend thus became less dangerous.

What helped Frank was the realization that he had been falsely blaming himself for his mother's unhappiness. Since he was not really the criminal, he didn't have to punish himself by holding himself back from having fun with others, especially his girlfriend.

DOING TO YOUR THERAPIST WHAT WAS DONE TO YOU

Another strategy you as a client may use is putting your therapist in the position you were in with your parents when they behaved badly towards you. You unconsciously want to evaluate your therapist's ability to deal with behavior that was difficult for you to deal with during childhood. Your goal is to learn from your therapist, just as you learn from others in life, how to better face the adversity of your past.

A client of mine named Hugh had a problem expressing his point of view or disagreeing with people. Hugh had been excessively criticized by his mother during his childhood. In therapy, he criticized me a lot, then closely observed how I reacted.

By seeing that I was not hurt by the same type of criticism that had hurt him, he became more secure. Why? By learning from my behavior how to face criticism, he felt more sure of himself.

Hugh could use my behavior as a model, be like me, and, by so doing, feel less hurt and provoked when criticized. Feeling less worried about criticism made it easier for Hugh to express his point of view. It also helped him to remember the painful experiences of having been criticized by his mother. He realized that because he had accepted his mother's criticisms, he thought badly of himself.

Arthur, another client who had a possessive mother, acted possessive towards me. He attempted to make me feel guilty when I went on vacation or canceled a session. "Don't you feel irresponsible, leaving your clients to deal their problems alone?" he asked. He wanted to see if I would act apologetic or angry at his remarks. This would be a sign that I suffered from the same sense of guilt his mother had made him feel when he attempted to be by himself or play with his friends. Arthur was relieved that I did not feel the need to explain or justify myself. I provided a model of how to deal with possessive behavior by his mother and others.

Another client, a man named David, had a father who would contemptuously dismiss his son's opinions as worthless, then pontificate endlessly. The son experienced this to mean that his father was insecure and easily threatened if he wasn't always right. As a result, in response to his father's weakness, David developed a destructive mind-set: "My opinions are threatening to my father, so I'd better stay in the shadows, think of myself as a loser, and not value my ideas." Living his life according to this mind-set resulted in academic failure, poor self-esteem, and excessive deference to others. In order to overcome this kind of behavior, David needed to safely face its origins. What did he do?

He acted contemptuous of me the way his father had acted toward him. He would say that he couldn't remember what I had said to him in our last session and that he felt uncomfortable about not paying more attention. When I asked about his discomfort, he acted relieved that I wasn't critical of him for not paying more attention to my ideas. I wasn't hurt as David had been when his father disregarded his point of view, and I therefore provided a model of how to face what had been traumatic for him. This helped him to feel safer and to begin facing a problem that developed in relation to his father.

David had just been notified that he had been given a large bonus, but somehow he had put off telling his wife about it.

I asked him why he had not told her. He said he felt it was wrong to brag about his success. That presented me with the opportunity to help him connect his problems with success with his father's need to be the only important person in the family.

WHEN A THERAPIST FAILS THE TEST

I once supervised Tim, a psychiatrist in training, who was treating a twenty-one-year-old student named Phil for depression and suicidal thoughts. In response to the sense of worry Phil stimulated in him, Tim reluctantly but continually gave in to Phil's demands for advice and medication. Tim told me that he was uncertain about taking this course of action because Phil wasn't improving. However, he was afraid not to agree to Phil's demands because he feared Phil might kill himself.

Responding to the information that Phil was not improving, I recommended Tim stop agreeing to his demands and instead look into the reasons behind the demands. This advice helped Tim to worry less so that he could take a different approach with Phil. As a result, Phil became calmer, less demanding, and less depressed. Why?

Since the age of eight, Phil had been traumatized by his father's suffering and frequent brushes with death as a result of severe kidney disease. Phil worried a great deal about his father, which caused him to develop an excessive sense of responsibility for him. This impaired his ability to focus on his own life because to do so would mean to him that he was neglecting his father. Whenever his father did poorly, the son became anxious and depressed. In the period preceding his coming for help, Phil's father had become very depressed. Shortly afterward, the son also became depressed and sought help.

Phil displayed his suffering to his therapist by showing how needy he was for medication and advice. He was testing his therapist to see if he could resist rescuing someone who was suffering. The emotional pull on Tim was too strong for him to overcome.

When Tim failed the test by continuing to give advice, it made Phil feel worse because he did not have a model to show him how to face his father's suffering. Conversely, when Tim stopped giving advice, Phil, instead of feeling frustrated, felt relieved. He also began to recall how disturbing his father's illness had been, and the ways in which it hampered his life. If his therapist could overcome the provocation of Phil's suffering, Phil could do the same with his father.

A Sense of Security

The sense of security you acquire from having a good current role model makes achieving forbidden goals seem less dangerous. If your therapist is undeterred by hurtful behavior, you can be undeterred by it as well. This can help you to pursue the goals you thwarted as a child in response to your parents' and/or siblings' hurtful behavior. Learning by observing your therapist is similar to couples with very different personality traits learning from each other how to act differently in order to overcome self-defeating behavior.

One important advantage to treating your therapist the way you were treated, as opposed to putting him or her into the role of your parent or sibling, is that there is less risk of your being hurt again, because it is the therapist who is being mistreated. If you put the therapist in the parent role and he or she falls short, you may be hurt again as you were in childhood.

Human relationships would be so much better if people did unto others as they would like to have others do unto them. Instead, people do to others what was done to them. Remember, the advantage of being the doer of hurtful behavior, instead of the receiver of mistreatment, is that you don't have to remember what was painful in your past. Watching someone else suffer removes the focus from your own past suffering and helps to hide the pain that was inflicted on you. Now you are in the opposite position emotionally.

Additionally, the benefit of doing to others what was done to you is that in watching them respond you hope that they will be less perturbed by your behavior than you were when your parents treated you the same way. This would mean that that person has mind-sets that are different from the destructive ones you have developed in response to the same hurtful behavior. You hope to acquire similar mind-sets for yourself.

In recent years, the general public has become more aware of this mechanism as a result of the publicity surrounding child abuse cases where adults mistreat children the way they were mistreated. In the therapy situation, we have just seen how this mechanism is used by the client to change his or her behavior and to recover memories of the family events that caused the behavior.

The Client as Coach

If you as a client think that your therapist is a little off track or doesn't understand what you need to work on, you will often, without realizing it, coach him or her to behave in the correct way. You badly want your therapist to understand your problem and to respond appropriately, because the outcome is so important to you.

For example, if you have a problem giving in to authority, you might say to your therapist, "I know that you are not the kind of person who tells people what to do." In this instance you want the therapist to get the message to not be authoritarian or controlling.

A client of mine named Joy had been sexually abused by her stepfather and was not protected from the abuse by her mother. In her initial telephone call Joy wanted me to realize something about her anxieties and to demonstrate to her that I could approach them correctly.

She said, "A friend of mine recommended you highly. One thing I'm wondering is: As a psychoanalyst, do you always see clients several times a week?"

I thought that asking this right off instead of making an appointment to see me might mean that Joy was worried about our relationship becoming too intense. So I said, "That depends on what the two of us decide would be best. We might decide that one time per week or less often could be beneficial."

"Could you possibly recommend a female therapist for me?" she asked next. This was a clue that she might either be afraid of men or male therapists or be worried that I couldn't tolerate rejection.

I said, "Yes, I could recommend some women therapists for you if you would like."

"Well . . . if you don't mind, I'd like to think about it and get back to you," she said.

Again, realizing that her skittishness might mean that she was afraid to get stuck in a relationship, I said, "That's fine with me."

Joy seemed to need to feel that I wasn't upset about her being in control of our relationship and that I wouldn't be hurt if she chose someone else or decided not to see me at all. Without knowing it, she thus coached me to demonstrate to her that I could help her.

Once therapy began with me, Joy revealed that previously, while going to therapy three times per week, she had been traumatized by her male therapist falling in love with her. Before calling me for an appointment she had asked the client who recommended me if my stance with her was nonseductive. Even though my client had assured her it was, Joy still needed to check me out on her own before deciding to meet me.

Joy told me that both her stepfather and previous therapist had transgressed proper boundaries with her, causing her to suffer greatly. In light of this information, it was surprising to me that she did not choose a woman therapist, which on the face of it would have seemed safer for her. The explanation for this emerged later on. Joy felt that women were weak, like her mother, and therefore she worried that a woman therapist wouldn't be able to help her, since her mother had failed to protect her from her stepfather.

Changing in Therapy: The Ninety-Pound Weakling

In the old Charles Atlas comic book ads, a ninety-pound weakling on the beach had sand kicked in his face by a bully and lost his girl. Then he subscribed to the Atlas weight- and strength-training program. Later he returned to the beach with newly developed power and confidence, drove away the bully, and won back the girl.

In your life, an emotional bully has chased you away from pursuing what is important to you. *The more gains you make in your life, the stronger you become emotionally. When you are stronger, happier, and more successful, it is easier for you to face what was unpleasant in your past.* You can return to the beach, the scene of your former humiliation, so to speak. As you face what was unpleasant in the past, it becomes easier to recognize how you developed a mind-set that holds you back.

Although this may seem quite obvious to you on the surface, it is fundamental to understanding how you can change behavior you hate. As you achieve success in changing your attitudes and behavior, you will acquire a greater sense of confidence, which in turn makes it less painful to remember how you were mistreated in the past. In essence, you don't worry about returning to the beach. You are more confident about facing the bully.

The more you remember about past mistreatment and how you irrationally blamed yourself for it and held yourself back, the easier it is to continue making additional gains.

If you are not at fault, then you don't have to suffer. When you see that your parents' and/or siblings' destructive behavior towards you was independent of what you did, you will feel less self-blame and guilt, and therefore feel more justified to be happy. Just as if you had been been imprisoned unfairly and then released, you will feel justified to be free and to enjoy your life.

You can see this principle applied in everyday life. In new social or business situations we feel people out, looking for qualities we fear and admire, to better guide our own behavior. The more success we have, the less dangerous these situations seem. When we feel less endangered it becomes easier to do well in these situations, and therefore the better we do. If, for example, you are very concerned about rejection in dating, successes in dating will make it easier for you to be bolder in the future.

How Can You Tell if Therapy Is Working?

The most important way to determine whether your therapy is working is to evaluate how you are feeling. If you are feeling better, your therapy is working. If you came for help because you were depressed, your mood should be more upbeat. If you came because your relationship with your partner was bad, the relationship should be better, or you should have a clearer understanding of why it is not working. If you were unable to leave a bad marriage, after self-discovery and effort you should be clear about what went wrong and be able to end the marriage.

Getting better also includes a deeper awareness of what your problems are and what has caused them, but that is secondary to feeling better. If you felt ambivalent about your relationship, you should feel less so. If you had difficulty getting involved with the opposite sex, you should now be more successful. If you were ruining your career opportunities or not promoting yourself to get ahead, there should be more progress in that area. If you were always saying yes to people when you really wanted to say no, you should now be more decisive. If you were always saying no to people and were unable to say yes when you wanted to, you should now be freer to pursue your interests.

You don't have to make an intellectual assessment or evaluation of your therapist's skills. You need only to assess your progress. Are things getting better?

WHAT IF YOU FEEL THAT THERAPY IS NOT WORKING?

When therapy is not working, there are several things you can do. The most important one is to discuss the problem with your therapist and explain exactly what is bothering you. If, after discussing this for several sessions, your therapist does not arrive at an explanation that is satisfactory, or you notice no improvement, or you feel worse, get a second opinion from another therapist. If none of these things help, take the initiative and find another therapist.

If you hire a math tutor and your math skills don't improve over time, you need to find another tutor. If your stockbroker or investment counselor consistently loses money instead of making it, that person should be replaced. If you are a diabetic and you receive penicillin by mistake instead of insulin, you are going to get worse. If the mistake is not corrected, you must get another doctor.

You may think your therapist is a lovely person: kind, insightful, and brilliant. But if the problem you came for is not improving, your therapist is failing you.

Do not let yourself be influenced to continue in therapy with the same person as a result of the views of some therapists who believe that learning about yourself is the most important thing, even if it means you have to suffer. If your therapist truly understands why you behave in ways you hate, his or her explanations should make sense to you and help you to feel better.

In the process of feeling better and overcoming your problems, you will face unpleasant memories and feelings associated with your past. That is one of the ways you acquire knowledge about why you behave in ways you hate. Experiencing unpleasant memories and feelings should not be confused with getting worse.

Temporary emotional upsets that are connected with memories of a troubled past are to be expected. This is an indication that you are making progress. It means that your therapy is going in the right direction. Your therapist has obviously passed your tests of him or her, making it safe enough for you to face your past and to understand how your early experiences caused the behavior you hate.

These upsets should be short-lived, however, and should provide you with insight and perspective on why some of your current life situations are problematic. For example, you may feel anger and remorse when remembering experiences of rejection by your parents that caused you to feel distant from people later in life. That is an indication that your therapy is working, and it should lead to insight into your current problems and help you to feel more comfortable about getting closer to people. This is the most important criterion. You should be feeling closer to the people in your life. This tells you that you are growing stronger, like the former ninety-pound weakling, and feeling safer to return to the beach.

Other kinds of emotional tensions will occur when you behave toward your therapist the way you were treated, a mechanism we just discussed. If you were put down as a child, you may very well put down your therapist to see if he or she can handle it differently from the way you did. If one or both of your parents suffered in front of you, causing you to feel that you had to rescue them, you may suffer in front of your therapist to see if he or she needs to rescue you. If your therapist doesn't feel hurt when you put him or her down or doesn't need to rescue you when you suffer, you will feel relieved or calm. If you were having difficulty feeling happy because your parent or sibling was grimly depressed, you should start to feel happier.

No matter whether you come away with a million insights and ideas about your parents, siblings, friends, partner, boss, relatives, and others, if you are not feeling or doing better, your therapy is a failure. On the other hand, if you seem to acquire no insights but find your life improving significantly, then your therapy is working.

No matter what you have been told or have read, the best guide for judging the success of therapy is its outcome. If your life is better, the therapy is working. If your life is worse, it is not. Although this is the most important fact of all and should be obvious, it may be difficult for you to accept this principle, for reasons that we will discuss below. But if your life is still in turmoil after several months of therapy, you should find another therapist.

WHY IT MAY BE DIFFICULT FOR YOU TO LEAVE

For a number of reasons, you may find it difficult to leave if your therapy is going poorly. Perhaps you are caught up in what is fashionable in therapy at the moment and feel ashamed to admit that something supposedly so great has failed you. You may feel that it is your fault because you are not improving, especially if your therapist comes highly recommended.

The same mind-set that is responsible for the problems that caused you to seek therapy is responsible for making it difficult for you to speak up when your therapy is not working. For instance, are you feeling sorry for your therapist the way you might have felt with your mother, father, or a sibling? As a result, do you have to continue seeing your therapist no matter what? Are you afraid you will hurt his or her feelings if you complain or leave? Have you had a similar problem with having to protect some important person's feelings in the past?

Are you submitting to the authority of your therapist as you did with an overbearing parent or sibling? In other words, do you feel obligated to accept the word of your therapist that your therapy is going well, when your experience and intuition tell you differently? Perhaps your mind-set requires you to always let the other person be right in order to sustain his or her self-esteem. Did you have a family member who assigned that role to you?

Are you blaming yourself for not being a better client or for accepting a complaint from your therapist that you don't work hard enough? Are you afraid that your therapist will suffer financial loss if you leave? If so, in these cases are you repeating a pattern from your past of taking care of others at your own expense?

Just as your mind-sets interfered with your ability to see the truth about your relationships with your parents and siblings, they may cause the same problem to occur with your therapist. You may have to give your therapist a better grade than he or she deserves in order to feel you have not wasted your time and money. In addition, if you had a parent who too easily felt shame when his or her faults were exposed, you are likely to award your therapist an unjustified high grade to protect his or her self-esteem.

Like a primitive tribe, you may not have the perspective on cause and effect that you need to in order to realize why your therapy is not working. You may be acting as you did as a child and blaming yourself for the failure of your therapist. If so, guilt feelings, like an electronic dog collar, will cause you pain when you begin to think of leaving your therapist.

It is important for you to see that what has occurred in your therapy is not your fault. Just as there are mismatches between some children and parents, there are also mismatches between some clients and therapists. Since you now have more perspective about this situation, do something about it and save yourself needless suffering.

CHAPTER FOURTEEN

Solving Specific Problems in Therapy

HOW DOES PSYCHOTHERAPY HELP a person stop behaving in ways he or she hates? This chapter will explore the case study of Helen, a client of mine who used accommodation, rebellion, and mimicking to discover whether I had attitudes and motivations that were different from those of her parents.

Discovering that my attitudes were different from those of her parents helped Helen to remember the past experiences that led to her problem behavior. Placing me in the same difficult position she was in with her mother showed Helen how to successfully deal with problems that were difficult for her to overcome.

As this case study demonstrates, a client's progress is specifically connected with what the therapist says and does. By observing whether the client's goals are being achieved or delayed, the therapist will be able to assess his or her own skill or mistakes (see Chapter Thirteen for more details).

Woman on a Seesaw

When Helen first walked timidly into my office, she was overweight and dressed in unattractive, baggy clothes. She avoided eye contact, had an unflattering hair style, and wore no make-up. She was a twenty-five-year-old, single businesswoman who sought therapy because of her sense of inadequacy with men, difficulty asserting her opinions, and periodic bouts of depression, which had begun two years earlier. Helen was unaware of the causes of her depression. She thought its onset coincided with her leaving home to work in San Francisco.

Helen had just completed her M.B.A. She was plump but pretty, charming but shy, and cautious. She was tentative and uncomfortable when attempting to talk to me. Like a butterfly trapped in a cocoon long after it should have emerged, Helen was trapped by her mind-set.

I wondered what strategy she would use with me in order to deal with the problems she had come to solve.

In the first few months, Helen began to reveal how unsure she felt of herself. Essentially, she could not take any position without then thinking, saying, or doing the opposite. She described how she would express the wish to do something, then contradict herself by saying she didn't want to do it. She would say something favorable about herself and then cancel it by saying something unfavorable. She was uncomfortable expressing complaints or criticisms about people unless she offset them with compliments.

Helen was paralyzed when trying to be direct. She observed that she had displayed these qualities since childhood. She told me, "There is an obsessive side to me. When I was a kid, through adolescence, I'd be doing something and suddenly have a mental image of a string being wound up and then unwinding. It made me stop what I was doing at the moment." This childhood visualization always made it difficult for her to be forthright and to have a plan and follow through with it.

If I Go Up, They Go Down

When Helen discussed her female coworkers she was over-complimentary. In disagreements, she tended to defer to others. In the process of describing to me her thoughts about a work-related issue, she would vacillate, first telling me one thing, then characteristically saying, "I'm not sure that was a good idea."

Similarly, when making an observation about her own behavior, she would take it back, or defer to me by asking me what I thought. She said, "I feel I can't have anything without believing that I am taking it away from somebody else."

What was Helen's strategy in bringing up these concerns about her difficulties with her coworkers and her ambivalent behavior? What do you suppose she wanted me, as her therapist, to do about it?

She wanted to assess whether I was on the side of assertiveness and being direct, or whether I was more on the side of deferring to others. I pointed out that she seemed overly concerned about the women she worked with and that she seemed fearful of hurting or displacing them.

After I made this observation, she remembered a presentation she had made. She felt uncomfortable in spite of having been well prepared and having given a good presentation. To me this was evidence that I was on the right track. Helen was feeling safer, and therefore more encouraged to talk about her discomfort. I observed that she seemed to be afraid of being smart and well-informed because this would show that she knew more than her female coworkers. Did she think that was a problem?

She answered, "I'm afraid they will feel envious of me. Perhaps that explains why I felt depressed after a previous presentation where I showed that I knew my stuff."

Helen felt reassured because my observations encouraged her to show her competence, and therefore they implied that I would not be envious of her. If I was not envious of her success, she could feel secure enough to reveal that she worried about feeling envied. Her mind-set was "Showing my intelligence hurts other people; therefore, I must hide my intelligence." As Helen worked to overcome suppressing her intellect, there was a noticeable improvement of assertiveness at work and an increase in her directness with me.

As she addressed her behavior in the present, we started to examine the source of her problem. I believed that an important family member must have been threatened by Helen demonstrating her intelligence, competence, and directness. This had probably caused her to defer to others and to avoid being direct and overtly intelligent.

We Take a Sharp Turn

Instead of continuing to focus on problems at work, however, Helen's concerns in therapy now shifted to a very different but nevertheless important matter. She began to complain about her relationship with Dennis, her live-in boyfriend.

Dennis was less educated than Helen. He had children from a former marriage that he expected her to care for. Also, he expected her to be subservient to him and didn't pay his share of the expenses. When I attempted to explore this, she became irritable with me and complained that I was trying to control her life. Nonetheless, she continued to complain about her dissatisfaction with her boyfriend.

It seemed ironic to me that in spite of her complaints about Dennis, Helen was not considering ending their relationship. In fact, Helen continued to get more involved with him, even though I questioned whether this was what she really wanted. After a few months of this, I suggested that in view of her obvious doubts about Dennis and her difficulties with him she should not become more deeply committed to him until she understood more about what the relationship meant to her.

She responded with relief and began to entertain thoughts of leaving him and getting her own apartment. She said, "I guess if I did what I wanted to do and was happy, I would be showing up my mother and sister and proving that their lives are wasted."

She explained that neither her mother nor her sister was happy in her marriage. "When Mother complained about Father, I often thought that she could have gotten someone else,"she told me. *Helen had just revealed the mind-set that was responsible for her staying in a relationship that made her unhappy. She was afraid of being happier than her mother and sister.*

How Helen Evaluated My Ability to Help Her

Initially, Helen had tested me to see whether I had a positive attitude towards her ambition to do well at work, and to see whether I would be envious or threatened by it. This led to the revelation that she was worried about being happier than her mother and sister. Because she had been reassured that I supported her ambition, she then felt more comfortable facing a concern that was more serious to her—namely, the relationship she was unhappy in, but unable to leave.

Although Helen had complained that I was trying to control her life, I eventually recommended that she not become further involved with Dennis. My suspicion that she would not in fact experience my strong stance as an attempt to control her life proved true, because instead of being resentful and indignant toward me she was relieved. Why?

Because it meant that I, unlike her mother, was not threatened by the possibility of her having a successful relationship with a man she could admire. Taking the position that she not become more deeply involved with Dennis made her feel I was supportive of her having a positive relationship with a man. In addition, my stance helped her feel sufficiently secure to begin facing her relationship with her mother and sister, which prevented her from being successful and happy with men.

Helen went on to talk about her mother's dogmatic manner. She described how her mother talked in moralistic platitudes, implying that she was saintly and above reproach. In Helen's eyes, her mother's only deficiency was that she complained so much. All of her complaints were about Helen's father, because he swore, enjoyed drinking beer with his buddies, was a nonbeliever, and lacked both an education and sophistication.

Will Interpretation Work This Time?

This information provided me with the opportunity to discuss how her mother's attitude towards her father affected Helen and made her feel sorry for her mother. I suggested that Helen's relationship with Dennis enabled her to have a man she could feel contemptuous towards, just as her mother was contemptuous of her father. This way she wouldn't have to worry about her mother feeling envious of her for being better off.

Helen's initial concern was that her coworkers were envious of her success at work. Facing and solving that issue helped reveal the origins of her problem, which began with her mother and sister. Helen now felt encouraged to elaborate further on the problem of her mother's envy of her.

She recalled that in high school her mother had encouraged her to date a boy who had very little personality or spark. Helen's girlhood interpretation of this was that her mother didn't want her to have a man with a dynamic personality. She wanted Helen to have the same kind of man she had chosen for herself. As Helen explained, "For some reason I felt it was hard to choose someone I liked if my mother didn't like him."

I asked what had made a more favorable choice difficult for her.

"Mother was so moralistic and self-sacrificing. She always complained about working long hours for me in her store. It made me feel that I needed to please her and be there for her. Otherwise, I'd feel guilty for abandoning her when she needed me."

This second reason why Helen felt sorry for her mother also contributed to the difficulty Helen had being happy with a man: The understanding that she chose men she was unhappy with, as her mother had done, in order to protect her mother from feeling envious, helped Helen to face her conflicts about men in general.

Helen had maintained her tie to her mother by squelching her positive feelings for her father and by replacing them with the same disdain her mother felt. Doing so made her feel no better off than her mother. To further promote her relationship with her mother, Helen adopted her attitudes, mimicked her style, and regularly complimented her.

Helen Sees That I'm Not Like Her Mother

Just as Helen would always compliment her mother, she often complimented me. She seemed to want to make me feel good, but I suspected that she did not want me to need praise or admiration from her the way her mother did. I was being placed in the role her mother was in, and I was being manipulated to enjoy feeling admired and good about myself as a result of Helen's compliments (accommodation). It was important for me to resist the temptation to be flattered by her so she could continue to face the problems she had with her mother.

If I behaved like her mother and showed that I needed Helen's admiration, she would not be able to ultimately face separating from, and feeling superior to, her mother. Whenever I questioned why she was complimenting me, or asked her what had brought a compliment to her mind at that particular moment, she was relieved rather than offended or hurt. This freed her to feel that she did not have to boost my ego as she did her mother's. This freedom allowed Helen to continue to be independent and to pursue what made her happy. Consequently, she was able to eventually alter the mind-set that demanded she stay tied to her mother for her mother's sake.

A therapist will know he or she is on the right track if a client begins to overcome his or her inhibitions and/or remembers the historical causes of those inhibitions.

At this point, Helen's life was improving. She was more assertive at work, had ended her unhappy relationship with Dennis, and was beginning to understand the origins of her problems with her mother. Freed from the paralyzing mind-set of having to sustain her mother, Helen no longer blindly followed the paths determined by her early bad experiences.

When Helen put me in her mother's role, she was reassured by my comments and interpretations that I did not have the same expectations of her that her mother had had. She gave me opportunities to fail her, but grew stronger when I demonstrated behavior that was different from her mother's. As a result, she felt more encouraged to face and solve the problems that arose from their relationship. By recalling memories from her childhood about her mother, Helen was overcoming the mind-set that was sabotaging her life.

Why a Sexual Liaison with a Woman?

An important instance of difficulty separating from her mother occurred when Helen left home for college. She felt very anxious during that time, and shortly after that she had a brief sexual liaison with a woman. She was obviously embarrassed when she told me about this, and emphasized that she couldn't understand why it had occurred.

What did it serve for her to present this memory to me? There was a risk for her that I would interpret this incident as her wish to replace her mother with another woman, which would mean that I thought she needed her mother and couldn't survive without her. Also, this incident could be viewed as an opportunity for Helen to get further control over her wish to feel independent of her mother without feeling guilty about it.

After all, based on her experience with her mother, her life had been controlled by the requirements of the mind-set "Mother needs me to be with her, and to be like her, in order for her to be happy."

Neither of these interpretations seemed right to me. I suggested that the anxiety Helen experienced when she left home for college resulted from her worry that her mother would be unhappy without her and that the sexual liaison was her unconscious attempt to comfort her mother by proving that Helen was still available to her because she was not interested in men.

Helen expressed great relief at this interpretation and confirmed its legitimacy by telling me that she had indeed inhibited her experiences with men after leaving home. Because I had recognized the meaning of her anxiety and of the sexual experience provoked by her leaving home, Helen felt safer to pursue more independence. This was a stepping-stone to the next phase of her analysis.

Separating from Me

An important step in furthering her relationships with men resulted from Helen's interactions with me before her vacation. She claimed that she was unhappy and sad and was going to miss me. She apologized for taking a vacation and justified taking it on the basis of being exhausted. I suggested that she was feeling sad about leaving me in order to make me feel better, because she worried that I, like her mother, would be hurt by her independence.

Helen's mood brightened, and she began to experience more excitement when talking about her trip. This was an important confirmation to me that her therapy was on the right track. Otherwise, if she were truly sad and needy of me, my remarks that her sadness was for my sake would have intensified her sadness, not relieved it. She would have felt rejected that I wasn't sensitive to her.

Helen's response to my remarks helped to confirm for me what I had earlier believed. Her struggle was to free herself from her mother, not to intensify it. Part of that struggle lessened as she learned to be comfortable separating from me.

As we continued to discuss the mind-sets that had developed in Helen's childhood and how they were manifested in her therapy, she felt greater conviction that I didn't have the same expectations of her that her mother did. Not only was Helen feeling happier, but her understanding of her destructive mind-sets deepened as well. The more she realized that she was limiting herself to accommodate her mother, the more Helen was able to loosen her unwholesome ties to her mother.

On her return from vacation, Helen expressed her pleasure in the break from therapy. "I probably felt the same about leaving home. Yet I wouldn't allow myself to feel it. I thought I had to suffer in order to have a good time. I couldn't enjoy being alone and felt I had to justify everything I did."

The conscious awareness that she had to suffer in order to have a good time demonstrated that Helen had developed more control over feeling guilty toward her mother when she enjoyed herself. It implied that she no longer felt she had to suffer.

Helen Sees Her Father in a New Light

As we continued to examine Helen's mind-set in relation to her mother and the ways she tested me to confirm that I did not have the same expectations of her, positive changes occurred in Helen's attitude. She started to date more frequently and with men she liked. She was playful, funny, and occasionally flirtatious with me, and began to recall positive memories of her father. She also began to lose weight, dress more fashionably, use make-up, and experiment with new hair styles.

One day she said, "I wonder if I make more of an impression on you than other female clients? I want to know that I am special."

"Tell me more," I asked.

She said, "I'm having fun with you. It reminds me of my relationship with my father. He had a wonderful sense of humor and was very playful with me."

In another instance, she remembered thinking that she would be freer to pursue success with men if her mother were dead.

"Why?" I asked.

She replied, "Then I think that I wouldn't feel so guilty about it."

I asked her, "Why would that reduce your guilt?"

"It would make me feel less disloyal to my mother," she said.

The fact that she was able to voice thoughts such as these was a good indication to me that she had gained more control over her guilt feelings.

Gaining more control over her guilt freed Helen to pursue her interest in men. This was manifested by more and more positive memories about her father as well as the increase in her positive feelings toward me. She said, "Father had a strong sense of humor, and he was the only one in the family who had a sincere concern for me without strings attached."

I Make a Mistake

At this point, Helen evolved a new strategy to help her solve the problem of closeness with her father in particular and men in general. Her compliments on my looks and my skills as a therapist continued. These had always served her need to see whether my ego needed boosting. Therefore, I routinely declined them. Whereas earlier in the analysis she was relieved when I said that she flattered me in order to make me feel better, as she did with her mother, now she became resentful. Her upset made me realize that I had made a mistake.

I had misunderstood what Helen was trying to work on by overlooking a change in the direction of her analysis. The focus of her therapy had shifted from realizing how she had accommodated to her mother to feeling much more positive about her father. Unlike her mother, Helen's father had always had a sincere interest in her. The only way for me to get back on track was to keep that in focus and to pay attention to her next remarks.

She complained, "I was worried you couldn't take a compliment." I already knew from previous sessions that Helen felt it was wrong to accept compliments and admiration from her father because her mother had been contemptuous of him. Helen wanted to see if I could model accepting admiration from her so that she could feel more comfortable accepting admiration from her father. If I could feel good about doing this, so could she.

Helen was doing to me what had been done to her. She wanted to test me to see if I had the capacity to feel good about accepting admiration. When I understood this and began to accept her compliments graciously, she learned from me that it was all right to accept admiration. This helped her to continue to remember her positive feelings about her father.

Helen's first major strategy involved putting me in the role her mother was in, hoping that I wouldn't require that she admire me as her mother had (accommodation). Next, she put me in a role she had had difficulty with, namely, accepting admiration (doing to me what was done to her). She wanted me to show that I could accept her admiration, because she had not been able to do so with her father. Using my behavior as a model, she could begin to see her father in a better light.

Competing with Mother, Winning with Men

As Helen progressed, she was less susceptible to guilt feelings towards her mother, which made it possible for her to experience competitive feelings towards her mother and sister. This was positive, because it meant that Helen now felt more justified in pursuing what she wanted. She remembered feeling guilty that her mother worked evenings in her store, while she was alone having fun with her father.

She boasted that she now felt superior to her mother because she could enjoy men and sex and was better off than her married older sister, who was bogged down with children and envied Helen's ability to travel and live independently. Her boasting was a reflection of her accomplishment in changing her mind-sets.

Now Helen started using another strategy to get control over her feelings of superiority to her mother and sister. She began challenging my ideas from time to time, then would assess whether or not I felt diminished by her behavior. Whenever she disagreed with me, she expressed concern about hurting my feelings. Then she would wonder if her opinions were really worthwhile or intelligent.

I suggested that she was worried that I would be offended by her, which in turn caused her to question her ideas. My remarks assured her that I wasn't threatened by her confidence in questioning me. As a result, Helen continued to be more assertive. One day she remembered how her mother had always needed to be in control and to have people depend on her.

For the first time in therapy, Helen was able to comment on her mother's destructive behavior without feeling guilty or apologetic. As time passed, her apologizing and justifications decreased, and her dissatisfaction with men and anxiety about sex disappeared. I took these to be signs that Helen was less worried about being better off than her mother. She was pleased that she was dating attractive, intelligent men, and she began having orgasms for the first time in her life.

Helen's obsessional preoccupation with saying something and taking it back greatly lessened, and she became more active and successful professionally. She was promoted to a supervisory position and had some of her writing published.

An example of these changes is evident in some of her comments from this period: "I'm feeling very sexual, and I'm having sexual fantasies about my male supervisor. And I'm feeling competitive with my coworker, Mary, for his attention. In these fantasies I'm showing her that I can be more desirable to him than she can, just as I felt with Mother that I would be a better woman for my father."

Another example of Helen's progress was her telling me that she wanted to be admired by people of quality, "not the ordinary types like my mother and sister." This was not a sign of her disdain for others, but rather an indication that Helen had emerged from her cocoon. Remember how inhibited and self-effacing she was at the beginning of therapy? Helen was beginning to erase her old mind-set and replace it with a new one: "I don't have to limit my life because of my mother and sister."

At a staff party she danced seductively with some of the men and was then told by two of her coworkers how they were taken aback by how sexual she had become. "I have a really shapely body and plan to get more clothes to show it off. I don't care if Mary feels threatened by me. I was selfish, pleased with myself, ecstatic. I was sexy!"

Helen was extremely pleased with the results of our work together and was now considering ending therapy. However, she expressed confusion about the feelings she was having over leaving me. She wasn't sure whether what she felt was guilt or sadness. When I asked what thoughts occurred to her about this, she remembered leaving her mother to go to college. I said I thought she was feeling the same way about me and that made her feel guilty towards me. This was confirmed when she said, "When I come in sad now, and with problems, it is to preserve your role. I imagine you will feel sad when I leave you, so I'm turning it around and making myself feel sad. It is directly connected with my mother and my need to rescue her."

These observations about her motivations, made without help from me, were additional signs of Helen's progress. Her original inclination, based on her relationship with her mother, had been to wait for me to guide her, so that I, in her mother's role, could take credit for her advances.

Now that Helen was no longer worried about depriving me, or her mother, of being in control, she was able to be in control of her own life. She no longer felt the need to praise her mother and her coworkers excessively to make them feel more worthwhile, and was able to shine in social and business situations without feeling guilty.

The next strategy Helen used to face the problem of leaving me was to begin to feel rejected by me, even though my attitude and comments towards her had not changed. When I asked about this, she said, "It has to do with leaving my mother and you. I end up feeling that you are rejecting me instead of me feeling that I am rejecting you." If she felt rejected by me, it justified her leaving me. In other words, she punished herself in order to feel less guilty.

Helen's final problem in therapy involved her relationship with a professional man about whom she was increasingly serious. She wanted to end her therapy but thought that I would expect her to stay with me while the outcome of the relationship was being decided, so that I could have a role in the decision.

When I asked Helen what it would be like for her to end therapy without my knowing how her relationship turned out, she said that she thought it would be a relief for two reasons. First, she would be in control, and second, I would be spared hearing about how she was successful with a man superior to the one her mother had.

Soon after this, she expressed doubts about her boyfriend not being good enough. I said that I thought her motive for telling me this was to spare me from feeling envious of her relationship. She was obviously very happy with that interpretation, because it allowed her to tell me that she was glad to be leaving therapy.

Two years after Helen ended treatment with me, I received a letter from her saying that she had married and was very happy.

Conclusion

Our primary goal in life is always to fulfill our best destiny. We recognize that conflicts over which we have no control interfere with that fulfillment. I hope that in reading this book you've been able to identify and overcome some of the mind-sets that have led to behavior you hate.

With what you've learned, you can now enjoy your life and break the generational cycle of behavior imposed on you by your parents and/or siblings. You may want to reread the charts and your personality profiles from time to time, especially as your children grow and new problems emerge. But now you know that no matter how deeply hidden your mind-sets or how damaging your past, you can overcome your problems and stop behaving in ways you hate.

You now have the tools to uncover your hidden beliefs and to understand the destructive behavior they cause. You can overcome your past and create a new direction for your future. Go and do it!

APPENDIX

Charts

MISMATCHES IN CHILDHOOD

What You Are	You Accommodate and Inhibit Yourself	You Rebel and Protest	You Do to Others What Was Done to You
You are outgoing or overly expansive, but your laid-back parent is provoked.	You become subdued and introverted.	You become wild, outlandish, and uncontrolled.	You inhibit your children or others from being expressive and outgoing.
You are quiet, whereas your parent needs stimulation.	You feel you have to perform, entertain, or be outspoken.	You remain shy, withdrawn, and quiet.	You insist that your children or others perform for you. You become angry if they are quiet.
You are not affectionate or responsive enough to your parent's need to love you.	You feel you have to be overly affectionate and accept everything your parent offers.	You reject affection, closeness, and guidance from others	You are overly loving and baby your children.
You are the wrong sex. Your parent is very disappointed.	You inhibit your sexuality and act more like the opposite sex. You have low self-esteem.	You act hypermasculine if you are rejected for being a boy, and vice versa. Nothing is your fault.	You are disappointed with your child's sex. You are antagonistic to those of a particular sex.

You are laid back, but your parent demands achievement.	You feel driven to succeed and are anxious about exams and competing. You fear failing.	You deliberately do poorly at whatever your parent expects you to achieve.	You demand achievement from your children and are perfectionistic with others.
You are born disabled, and your parent is burdened, resentful, or ashamed.	You try to hide your deficiency at all costs, and you feel guilty about receiving help for your problem.	You flaunt your disability and try to shame your parents.	You are insensitive to suffering in others. You make fun of people's deficiencies.
You're adventurous, but your parent is overprotective and fearful of danger.	You become cautious and inhibited about sports, activities, and new situations.	You throw caution to the wind, become a risk taker, and use poor judgment about dangerous situations.	You are overprotective with your children and worry about danger everywhere.
You are delightful, but your parent is indifferent or jealous.	You act subdued, avoid the limelight, and defer to others.	You refuse to give credit to others. You go out of your way to get recognition.	You are indifferent to the achievements of others.

HOW YOU CREATE NEW MORAL COMMANDMENTS

The Behavior of Your Parents or Siblings	They Are Hurt and Disturbed	Your Mind-Set Thoughts to Please Them Are	Your New Moral Commands Are
They are authoritative and need to be in control.	When you act independently and defy their authority.	"It is best to follow their rules and to do what I am told."	Obedience is good.
They are rejecting when you want to be close or affectionate.	When you want to be close or have other needs to be taken care of.	"It is wrong to be dependent, close, or intimate with them."	Independence is good.
They are possessive and need you to be involved with them over others.	When you are involved with or think highly of other people.	"It is wrong to be separate, keep my distance from them, or value others highly."	Loyalty is good.
They are self-centered and competitive with you.	When you try to be noticed, admired, or successful.	"It is wrong to stand out or to be accomplished."	Modesty and restraint are good.
They are depressed and needy.	When you don't sacrifice for them, take care of them, or feel sorry for them.	"It is wrong to focus on making myself happy."	Saving and rescuing the downtrodden are good.
They are failing in school or work.	When you are doing well.	"It is wrong to succeed and outdo them."	Being nice to others is good.
They live through your accomplishments.	When you fail to succeed or stand out.	"It is wrong to fail or make mistakes. It is wrong to not drive myself."	Success is everything.

They are unpredictable. They use drugs or alcohol.	When you speak up to confront them or demand reliability.	"Don't make demands or expect parenting."	Self-reliance and control are best.
They are overly critical.	When you refuse to accept blame.	"I'm at fault whatever the criticism."	Be perfect. Never make mistakes.
They are overprotective.	When you are wild, take chances, or are reckless.	"It is wrong to be adventurous."	Caution is best.
They are underprotective.	When you are watchful, wary, and cautious.	"It is wrong to be cautious."	Risk is good.
They are amoral.	When you do what is right and honest.	"It is wrong to be moral."	Dishonesty is best. Get what you want, no matter what. The ends justify the means.
They are very self-righteous, moralistic, and disdainful.	When you don't follow the straight and narrow.	"It is wrong to disobey the rules or cause them shame."	Righteousness above all.

HOW TO DISCOVER THE CAUSE OF YOUR PROBLEMS

Your Parent or Sibling Is	When You Accommodate to Their Bad Behavior	When You Rebel and Protest Against What They Expect	When You Become Like Your Parent and Do to Others What Was Done to You
Controlling and authoritarian	You overrespect authority, are conservative, unspontaneous, and obey the rules.	You are stubborn, resist demands, and refuse to give in. Your values conflict with theirs.	You are bossy, demanding, and controlling and expect strict obedience to you and the rules.
Rejecting	You are self-reliant and avoid needing people. You avoid showing feelings. Closeness to others feels risky.	You insist on having your demands met. You may act destructively to get attention.	You are indifferent to others and enjoy seeing them hurt or hurting them yourself.
Physically abusive	You feel unworthy and guilt-ridden. You will do anything to please.	You try to fight back as long as possible. You become rebellious and angry and have a chip on your shoulder.	You physically abuse others the way you were abused.
Possessive	You are overly loyal and feel afraid of being separate.	You reject demands made on you. You keep your distance from people who want to be close to you. You fear being taken advantage of.	You suffocate others. You feel jealous of attention paid to others. You may become violent in a jealous rage.

Your Parent or Sibling Is	When You Accommodate to Their Bad Behavior	When You Rebel and Protest Against What They Expect	When You Become Like Your Parent and Do to Others What Was Done to You
Competitive and self-centered	You are afraid to speak up or be the center of attention. You frustrate your successes and accomplishments.	You refuse to give credit to others' accomplishments. You go out of your way to get recognition and attention.	You put others down and enjoy their faults and failures. You need to be the center of attention.
Depressed and needy	You feel guilty about being happy. You tend to feel sorry for and rescue the needy. You have to help others before you can feel good.	You keep distant from anyone who is needy and unhappy. You become insensitive to others.	No one can please you. You suffer and complain all the time. You feel and appear grim to others.
Weak and ineffectual	You may feel that you have to be strong, take charge, act decisively.	You ignore problems in others and let them flounder.	You have no backbone. You are meek and give in to what others want.
Living through your accomplishments	You feel great pressure to do well or be perfect. You have to stand out. You fear failure. You feel anxious when you try to relax.	You hide your accomplishments and live an understated life. You deliberately fail.	You use people and take credit for what they do. You expect perfection and are overly critical of mistakes in others.

On alcohol or drugs and is unpredictable and/or violent	You become vigilant and alert. You will inhibit yourself to avoid setting them off. You will feel unprotected and insecure and have to be the parent.	You act hateful towards anyone not in control. You may become insensitive to suffering in others.	You are unpredictable, explosive, and unreliable. You will probably become a drug user.
Critical	You have low self-esteem, accept blame easily, have self-critical thoughts (I'm lazy, selfish, no good, etc.). You may feel there is no use trying.	You are feisty and rebellious and deny anything is ever your fault.	You are quick to blame others even when they have done no wrong.
Overprotective	You become very cautious. You are inhibited participating in sports and physical activities.	You are careless, reckless, and don't pay attention to danger. You use poor judgment about taking risks.	You are very restrictive towards others, especially your children. You see danger everywhere.
Underprotective	You take unnecessary chances and let yourself become exposed to danger. You don't notice the usual warning signs of trouble.	You become overly cautious and can't have fun easily. You are overly alert to possible trouble in most situations.	With your children and others, you tend to ignore signs of danger and allow others to endanger themselves.
Overly righteous and disdainful of others	You highlight your moral failings. You may get in trouble with the authorities.	You parade your moral virtues.	You are disdainful of and gloat about faults in others. You search them out.
Amoral or sociopathic	You have trouble following the rules and doing the right thing.	You insist on honesty in all your dealings and are intolerant of crooks and cheaters.	You use people and get what you want whatever the means.

HOW YOUR PARENT'S BEHAVIOR LEADS TO THOUGHTS YOU MAY HATE

Your Parent or Sibling Is	When You Accommodate You Think	When You Rebel and Feel Guilty, You May Accept Their Criticisms of You	When You Act Like Them You Think
Controlling and authoritarian	"Obedience is good." "Respect your elders." "Parents know best." "God and country above all."	"I'm just stubborn as a mule." "I can't do anything right." "Who do I think I am?"	"Do what I say." "Follow the rules." "You think you know it all."
Rejecting	"Self-reliance is best." "Showing feelings is weak." "Don't depend on others."	"I'm too needy." "I'm too emotional." "I'm just a baby."	"Don't bother me." "Keep your feelings to yourself." "I'm too busy."
Possessive	"Loyalty is good." "Stay away from strangers." "Blood is thicker than water."	"I'm just a flirt." "I'm a traitor." "I don't think of anyone but myself."	"How come you never call or write?" "After all I have done for you." "No one is good enough for you."
Overprotective	"Caution is good." "The world is a dangerous place."	"I'm so careless." "I never watch where I'm going." "I throw caution to the wind."	"You're going to kill yourself." "Watch your step." "Where are you going?"

Competitive and self-centered	"Modesty is good." "Don't be seen, don't be heard." "The meek shall inherit the earth."	"I'm a smart ass." "I'm a show off." "Who do I think I am?" "I'm stupid, ugly, and phony."	"I know best." "I'm great and wonderful." "Look how stupid and disgusting they are." "You think you know it all."
Depressed and needy	"Compassion is best." "Save the poor and downtrodden." "You poor thing." "What can I do to help?"	"I'm too insensitive." "I'm selfish." "I don't think of others."	"Woe is me." "Everything is terrible." "Life is such a problem." "What's the point of living?"
Living through your accomplishments	"Perfection is good." "Succeed at all costs." "My job is never done." "I'll never fail."	"I can't do anything right." "I'm a bum." "I'm a disappointment."	"It's not good enough." "Why can't you get all A's?" "It's not your best."
Unpredictable, uses drugs or alcohol	"Vigilance is best." "Never relax." "I'd better watch my step."	"I'm too blasé." "I have my head in the sand."	"Life is one big party." "Who cares, let's have fun." "Live for the moment."

EXAMPLES OF DOUBLE TROUBLE

Parent or Sibling A	Parent or Sibling B
Needs you to succeed to feel good. Lives through your accomplishments (looks, sports, grades, popularity).	Is competitive with you and is threatened by your success.
Is depressed and needy. You are overly attentive and worried about him or her.	Feels left out or rejected by your attention to the other parent.
Is rejecting toward you when you try to be close to him or her, causing you to become distant and self-contained.	Enjoys closeness and feels hurt by your aloof and distant attitude.
Wants you to be independent and strong.	Is possessive and upset by your independence from them. Wants to be able to baby you.
Prefers boys over girls. If you are a boy, you make this parent happy but displease the other.	Prefers girls over boys. If you are a boy, you will disappoint this parent.
Can't stand weakness or failure.	Can't stand strength.
Is emotionally explosive or labile. Drugs or alcohol may be involved. You become vigilant and worried about them.	Feels burdened by your vigilance and worry towards the other parent or towards him- or herself.
Is a failure, causing you to feel sorry for him or her. You fear doing well in life.	Lives through your accomplishments. Needs for you to be successful.

Your Symptom or Problem	Your symptom is a result of trying to not hurt or threaten your parent or sibling.	Your symptom is a rebellion or protest against what they expect of you.	You mimic your parent or sibling. You don't feel you deserve to be better off than they.
You overeat and are overweight.	1. They are unattractive, insecure about their looks and weight, and jealous of those who are attractive. Thus they are competitive with you. 2. They need you to eat in order to feel fulfilled.	1. Your parent (or sib) is overly worried about your eating habits or choices of food. They need you to be thin. 2. They may have withheld desserts as punishment.	Your parent (or sib) overeats and is overweight.
You are a failure in business, career, and at making money. You may be a gambler.	They are insecure about money and are jealous of wealthy and successful people. They brag about their skill with money.	Your parent (or sib) strongly needs you to be successful and wealthy in order to feel fulfilled in life.	Your parent (or sib) has failed in their career, business, or at making money. They may have been gamblers.
You feel insecure and inadequate without cause.	Your parent (or sib) has excessive pride and needs to show off and brag in order to feel worthwhile.	Your parent (or sib) needs you to be strong and independent. You protest by being insecure.	Your parent (or sib) is insecure and inadequate.
You have to show off and be the center of attention.	Your parent (or sib) feels inadequate and lives through your achievements to feel self-esteem.	Your parent (or sib) prefers that you be shy and retiring. He or she detests people who show off.	Your parent (or sib) is self-centered and has to show off.

219

Your Symptom or Problem	Your symptom is a result of trying to not hurt or threaten your parent or sibling.	Your symptom is a rebellion or protest against what they expect of you.	You mimic your parent or sibling. You don't feel you deserve to be better off than they.
You suffer and complain all the time.	They resent your sense of well-being and need to feel superior.	Your parent (or sib) expects you to keep your pain and problems to yourself.	Your parent (or sib) complained, suffered, and acted like a victim.
You are compliant and do what you are told. You are a yes-man. You strictly follow the rules.	Your parent (or sib) is authoritarian and controlling, and possibly rigid.	Your parent (or sib) wants you to be a rebel or a nonconformist, or they are rebellious nonconformists.	Your parent (or sib) does what he or she is told, and is a yes-man.
You are shy and avoid the limelight.	Your parent (or sib) needs to be the center of attention.	Your parent (or sib) wants you to perform and be center stage.	Your parent (or sib) is shy and avoids the limelight.
You avoid closeness with others.	1. Your parent (or sib) is rejecting towards you and/or burdened by closeness. 2. The parent of the same sex competes with you for the other parent.	Your parent (or sib) is possessive and wants you to only be close to them.	Your parent (or sib) avoids closeness with others.
You are dependent and needy.	Your parent needs to mother or baby you.	Your parent (or sib) is rejecting. Your parent (or sib) wants you to keep your distance from him or her.	Your parent (or sib) is dependent and needy.

You have to be right.	Your parent (or sib) lives through your intellectual achievements.	They are ... or usually wrong.	...about life.
You compulsively yell.	They need to feel superior by always being in control.	1. They didn't pay attention to you. 2. They couldn't tolerate any expression of emotion.	They yelled all the time.
You steal or cheat.	They need to feel morally superior and righteous.	They deprived you, cheated you, used you.	They are dishonest and cheat and steal.
You are excessively mistrustful of others.	They expect you to trust and depend only on them.	They are naive and overly trusting. They are easily taken advantage of.	They are mistrustful or paranoid.
You have many affairs but run the other way when the other person falls in love with you.	1. The parent of the same sex competes with you for the other parent. 2. Your parent (or sib) was very rejecting 3. Your parent (or sib) lives vicariously through your sexual conquests.	1. Your parent (or sib) was too involved with you, making you feel smothered or trapped. 2. They were overly moralistic about sex.	Your parent (or sib) had many affairs and was uncomfortable showing affection to his or her spouse.
You choose partners who reject you.	A parent (or sib) is jealous, hurt, and rejected by your relationship with the other parent or other people.	Your parent (or sib) needs you to have ideal, blissful relationships with others.	Your parent, usually of the same sex, is rejected by the other parent.
You are self-reliant and avoid showing your feelings.	Your parent (or sib) is rejecting and lacks sympathy and empathy for you.	Your parent (or sib) is overly depressed and needy of sympathy and caring.	Your parent (or sib) is indifferent to the suffering or needs of others.

221

CHECKING OUT YOUR SYMPTOMS, Continued

Your Symptom or Problem	Your symptom is a result of trying to not hurt or threaten your parent or sibling.	Your symptom is a rebellion or protest against what they expect of you.	You mimic your parent (or sibling). You don't feel you deserve to be better off than they.
You are a rescuer and over-sensitive to people in need.	Your parent (or sib) is needy, unhappy, or mistreated. Requires attention from you.	Your parent (or sib) is indifferent to suffering.	Your parent (or sib) is a rescuer and do-gooder.
You please and accommodate others. You give in too easily.	Your parent (or sib) is very demanding and authoritarian, or needy and guilt-provoking.	Your parent (or sib) wants you to be stubborn and uncooperative.	Your parent (or sib) pleases and accommodates others.
You are perfectionistic and are never satisfied with your accomplishments.	Your parent (or sib) lives through your accomplishments, but is never satisfied with them.	Your parent (or sib) wants you to fail or makes fun of you when you make mistakes, is competitive with you.	Your parent (or sib) has to be perfect.
You are extremely vigilant, worried, and insecure.	Your parent (or sib) uses drugs, alcohol, or is mentally unstable and unpredictable.	Your parent (or sib) is in denial whenever a crisis occurs.	Your parent (or sib) is anxious, vigilant, or worried.
You are a liar.	Your parent (or sib) needs to look good and feel good. He or she is vulnerable to the truth.	1. Your parent (or sib) is moralistic or rigid about telling the truth. 2. Your parent (or sib) is critical and finds fault with you.	Your parent (or sib) never tells the truth.

PROBLEMS WITH YOUR CHILDREN

What You Do to Them	They Do to You What You Did to Them	They Rebel or Protest	They Accommodate
You are critical of them.	They are critical of you.	They deny your accusations and refuse to listen to your suggestions.	They accept your criticisms and accuse themselves. "I'm selfish, no good, lazy, rotten, dishonest, etc."
You are perfectionistic with them. You live through their accomplishments.	They are perfectionistic with you. In their eyes you always fall short.	They are sloppy, careless, and may refuse to compete.	They are driven to succeed but anxious when performing (fear of failure).
You are controlling and authoritarian.	They are controlling and demanding with you.	They are defiant, rebellious, and passive-aggressive.	They are submissive, obedient, and meek.
You act rejecting of them.	They reject you.	They demand attention at any cost to themselves.	They control their feelings of need for affection.
You are possessive of them.	They are possessive towards you.	They stay away from you and keep emotional distance from you.	They cling to you and have trouble leaving home (school phobia).
You are depressed or needy with them.	They are depressed and needy around you.	They are indifferent to complaints or suffering.	They are overly attentive to you. They go overboard to make you happy.

PROBLEMS WITH YOUR CHILDREN, Continued

What You Do to Your Children	Your Children Do to You What You Did to Them	Your Children Rebel or Protest	Your Children Accommodate
You are focused on yourself and have to be the center of attention.	They are self-centered and focus attention on themselves.	They never give you credit for your accomplishments.	They stay in the background and avoid showing what they can do.
You are submissive and usually give in.	They are submissive and give in.	They are stubborn and refuse to give in.	They take charge and make decisions for you.
You are abusive to them.	They are abusive towards you or others.	If possible, they fight back. They become rebellious and antisocial.	They become fearful, withdrawn, sullen, depressed, or spaced out.
You are shy.	They are shy.	They take center stage.	They try to bring you out.
You are overprotective.	They express an extreme worry about you getting hurt.	They take unnecessary chances and expose themselves to danger. They are known as daredevils.	They become overly cautious about sports and other activities. They worry about getting injured.
You are underprotective.	They ignore you when you or their siblings are in danger; for example, if you are drunk and want to go for a drive.	They become overly cautious and can't easily have fun.	They take chances and expose themselves to danger.

You are dishonest in your dealings with people.	They lie, cheat, and steal excessively.	They become overly concerned with doing the right thing, to the point of moral righteousness.	They have trouble following the rules and doing right by people.
You are righteous and disdainful of others.	They act morally superior to you and point out your faults.	They will highlight their failures, get into trouble, and become antisocial.	They will highlight their virtues and act contemptuous of others.
You abuse drugs and alcohol. You may be unreliable, unpredictable, and/or violent.	They abuse drugs, become erratic, unreliable, and possibly violent.	They act hateful towards you or anyone on drugs and not in control. They may become insensitive to suffering in others.	They become vigilant and alert and act parental towards you. They feel anxious and inhibit themselves to avoid setting you off.

INDEX